With Interviews from the Fox Broadcasting Company Special
Bill Couturié and Nicholas Pileggi, Executive Producers
Bill Jersey and Janet Mercer, Producers
Pete Hamill, Original Story

A LOOKOUT BOOK

LOYALTY AND BETRAYA

THE STORY OF THE AMERICAN MO

S I D N E Y   Z I O

CollinsPublishersSanFrancisco

Contents

Millions of immigrants landed at Ellis Island at the turn of the

century with dreams as large as their knapsacks were scrawny. The New World beckoned, and with it the promise of a better life for them and their children.

A few came bearing nightmares. They had their eyes on easy street—and other people's gold. Small-time thugs, petty thieves, they followed their prey from the slums of Dublin, Palermo and Minsk, and stole from them as they had in the Old Country.

The mean streets of the new ghettos spawned their youth brigade, and given the dismal poverty, the wonder is that so few of the children turned to crime. Like the slums, crime was primitive and disorganized in the early years of the century—and might well have remained so, had America not gone to war against the demon rum.

Prohibition, the Noble Experiment, turned America into a giant speakeasy, ushered in the Jazz Age and turned its pug-ugly gangsters into bootleggers, who overnight got themselves rich and on a first-name basis with doctors, lawyers, bankers, businessmen, judges and politicians.

By the late '20s, Prohibition had created organized crime in America. Now it was not only booze, it was gambling and rackets such as loan-sharking.

Most people saw the mobsters as lovable rogues, Damon Runyon's guys and dolls, who somehow kept street crime under wraps and allowed tenement doors and windows from Harlem to the Bowery to remain unlocked, forget about unbarred.

The Mob provided millions of satisfied customers with everything from hooch to theater tickets. They lent cash when the banks said no. They provided businessmen with the unions of their choice and the unions with the goons of their choice. For half a century they gave us these things, and they, of course, gave us Las Vegas, the point spread and double-breasted pin-striped suits.

Most important, the Mob's rule lasted long enough for many of the young cops and lawyers they bribed and hired during the Depression to become inspectors, assemblymen, congressmen, senators, judges and mayors in the years ahead.

It was a system that worked, its survivors tell us, because of loyalty. A loyalty fed by fear and self-interest, to be sure, but nonetheless a loyalty that kept the law from the door. You got caught, you didn't blow the whistle.

Death before dishonor was the way of the underworld, *omerta* its First Commandment. For at least four generations, the Mob remained a highly restrictive, secretive business, a confederation of blood-oaths that had the power of young love.

And then it was over.

Loyalty turned into betrayal.

It happened, just as it always seems to happen: when you think you're on top of the world and nothing can happen. At the dawn of the '60s, the Mob was in clover, harvesting its long years of corrupting politicians and cops and district attorneys.

Then came narcotics and with that, rebellion.

Robert F. Kennedy emerged as the Mob's Public Enemy Number One and soon surfaced its first major informer in the person of Joe Valachi, a New York button man, who chose to ditch *omerta* when faced with life in prison.

His sing song made the FBI finally admit that organized crime existed in America, and the Mob's free ride was on its way out.

Soon the closed, old world, multiethnic confederation of Godfathers was replaced by a violent breed of spoiled disco brats who scoffed at the old rules, shot up their elders and grabbed the drug money as if it were cotton candy.

And it was drug traffic that spread chaos among the hierarchy and placed the Mob in Chapter Eleven. Where a canary once upon a time was a rara avis, where a four-star general like Lepke Buchalter went to the chair rather than talk, the current generation of wiseguys queue up for the *David Letterman Show*. *Omerta* can't keep its mouth shut, let's face it.

Today, there's a special FBI unit assigned to keep up with the comings and goings of 5,000 mobsters in the Federal Witness Protection Program.

The mafiosi who live in this new world, as if they were in the YMCA, got there by choosing a tape recorder over a bullet behind the ear. And with more enthusiasm than Bobby Kennedy could ever have imagined. They are not only telling us about their hits and misses, they're describing a society—like Incas thawed out of a deep freeze, laying on tales from a distant world we had only conceived of in the movie houses of our minds. You can read about it all here, from the mouths of such folk as Phil Leonetti, the ex-underboss of Philadelphia; Dominick Montiglio, former Gambino associate; and Billy Beattie, the Westie who was the Irish butcher to the Mob.

Their stories are as riveting as a public hanging—and just as entertaining. ★

Chapter One
New World, Old Woes

Having endured their Atlantic crossing, late-19th-century immigrants had but a ferry ride left from Ellis Island to New York City—where they found not gold, but a grinding poverty that was depressingly familiar.

BETWEEN BUILDINGS
*that loomed like mountains we
struggled with our bundles,
through the swarming streets of
the ghetto. I looked about the
narrow streets of squeezed-in
stores and houses, ragged clothes,
dirty bedding oozing out of the
windows, ash cans and garbage
cans cluttering the sidewalks.
A vague sadness pressed down
my heart, the first doubt of
America. I looked out into the
alley below, and saw pale-faced
children scrambling in the
gutter. "Where is America?"
cried my heart.*
     —ANZIA YEZIERSKA
    *young girl arriving in New York City
            from Russia*

School was a luxury for turn-of-the-century immigrant children. Some entered factories, mines and sweatshops as early as age 5.

The Promised Land

IF SLUMS ARE CRIME SCHOOLS, the Lower East Side of New York City in the early days of the 20th century was Harvard. Its rat-infested tenements were the dormitories, its teeming streets the campus of a university whose alumni dominate the Hall of Fame of Crime: Lucky Luciano, Meyer Lansky, Johnny Torrio, Bugsy Siegel, Frankie Yale, Lepke & Gurrah, Joe (the Boss) Masseria, Waxey Gordon, Monk Eastman and Dopey Benny Fein.

Future stars were attracted from other parts of town, most notably Frank Costello, Al Capone, Dutch Schultz and Owney Madden—and, of course, the school spawned hundreds of adjunct scholars who specialized in garroting, head smashing and the supporting arts; not to mention the countless independents who majored in pickpocketing, pushcart dumping and other sciences.

The faculty grew out of the mean streets, with one extraordinary exception: Arnold Rothstein. Rothstein was uptown, his father was known as Abe the Just, one of the great cotton manufacturers of New York.

Arnold Rothstein, the black sheep of a fine German-Jewish family, was the dean of the school. F. Scott Fitzgerald would feature him in *The Great Gatsby* as the man who fixed the World Series of 1919. A. R., as he was always known, taught the boys from downtown how to work, how to make something of themselves, how to flourish, how to dress.

But crime is homegrown, and looking back on it today, one can only wonder why so few out of the millions who grew up in the slums of the Promised Land turned to it.

The city was a "devil's dream," Mike Gold wrote about his childhood on the Lower East Side, "where flowers could not grow, but the rose of syphilis bloomed by night and day."

Yet out of this flowerless ghetto, packed with immigrants from Italy, Russia, Poland, Ireland, China—New York and America bloomed. Irving Berlin came out of this milieu, and Fannie Brice, and much of what became the great music and theater, the literature and sciences that stand as the signature of the American Century.

Lawyers, judges, writers, business tycoons, media moguls trace their origins to the Lower East Side—and the slums of Chicago, St. Louis, New Orleans, you name it. Politicians also, some of them good, and statesmen and professors.

But we remember the criminals and the crime. And the crime was primitive. The alumni who made the Hall of Fame began no differently from the faceless drones we shall never recall. They were petty thieves, they were bashers of laborers, they were killers. They were without the philosophical depth of the Godfather.

They cut across religious and ethnic lines. The Irish gangs held the slums earlier and now had graduated to Tammany Hall, the legit mob. The Italians, who get most of the grief today, were the next, and then the Jews. The WASPs had already stolen the country where it counted—the railroads, the industries, Wall Street—and this long before the "immigrant scum" showed up on America's shores, showed up because the WASPs needed cheap labor and the "scum" needed to save their lives from tyranny.

Crime was local in the early days of the century, organized loosely and only on ethnic grounds. Joe the Boss ran Little Italy, Dopey Benny Fein had the Jewish quarter, the Irish ran the West Side and, of course, Tammany. Arnold Rothstein tried to teach them to keep from killing each other off, but even the great A. R. was unable to deter these bad boys from fouling each other's nests.

The Mafia was in its infancy here, mainly Black Hand crews and guys running the Italian lottery. The Jewish gangs worked the union lines and gambling and were quite as brutal as the mafiosi and the Irish.

But all of this stuff, in New York and everywhere that slums existed, was as nothing next to the music that was playing in the great world of Christian temperance. Carry Nation, Billy Sunday and the Anti-Saloon League were out to destroy the demon rum—and in the doing, they created organized crime in America.

"Prohibition is better than no booze at all," Ring Lardner said. And the Mob rolled in and rolled on. ★

A Tinderbox Ready to Burn

In the 1880s, immigrant ghettos like New York City's Lower East Side were hardly the romantic paradises remembered by Hollywood and in the nostalgic family tales passed down through the generations. No one lived in these hellholes by choice. But lacking money and contacts (not to mention, among the post-Irish newcomers, a command of the English language), they had few options except to work menial jobs in order to afford the exorbitant rents being charged for a room or two in a squalid slum. Add to this an ingrained Old World fear of law enforcement agencies, and conditions were ripe for the emergence of ruthless immigrant gangs that preyed on their own.

I ASKED MOE HOW HE *ever started making so much money. And he said, "Well, down in the Bowery, there were push-carts all along the way," and he said, "We used to have other gangs, Irish gangs, Italian gangs and everything. But we, the Jewish kids, charged the pushcart dealers a dollar, and we would keep all the other gangs from stealing off their pushcarts." He never told me they had any trouble collecting. They worked in a cherry factory picking pits out of cherries. But they didn't like that. That's why they started charging the dollar to the pushcarts. They just seemed to go along with it because they were never bothered after they started paying the dollar. Ben Siegel was always behind everybody. Ben was like the protector. He was the first one to fight. 'Course, they all had to fight. Even Meyer had a fistfight all the time. And Moey had a fist fight. You had to prove yourself or you weren't in it. If somebody had to be shot, nobody had to ask anybody because Ben was always in back saving everybody's back. And that's why, especially our little mob—later I realized it was my little mob too—that's why we were against the bad guys and we all stuck together. We were supposed to be our individual family, and that's how we wound up.*

—BEATRICE SEDWAY
*widow of Moe Sedway,
Bugsy Siegel associate*

Steam grates often heated more reliably than tenement radiators.

Uptown swells could get rich by exploiting off-the-boat immigrants.

Same City, Different Planet

It was an age gilded by the dawn of modern technology: heavier-than-air machines that flew and buildings that scraped the sky; Bell's gadget to talk across the miles and Ford's Model Ts to drive them. It was, in short, a splendid age to be a mainstream American of means. Yet each of the nation's great metropolises also had enclaves crowded with both immigrants (landing, by 1910, at the rate of one million a year) and blacks fleeing northward. To these dispossessed, the riches of uptown seemed as unattainable as that diamond ring behind the bulletproof window. Wrote the reformer Jacob Riis: "The boy who steals fifty cents is sent to the house of correction. The man who steals a railroad goes free. So, every street child is a born gambler. He has nothing to lose, and all to win." Small wonder the underworld winners proved as cruel as the asphalt jungles from which they emerged.

Toasting the bride-to-be, 1905

08: Families shared alley houses in Washington, D.C.'s now-tony Dupont Circle.

The joys of robber barony: the Vanderbilt mansion on New York City's Fifth Avenue

1911, the prostitutes of Chicago—from $1-a-tricksters to $500-a-nighters—all tithed to the Mob.

Sweatshops didn't look for skills—just hunger and a willingness to swallow pride.

A Preemptive

Exploited day laborers helped fuel the union movement.

In 1911, the Triangle Shirtwaist Factory in downtown Manhattan caught fire; 141 workers, nearly all Jewish immigrants, perished because the owner had locked every exit. It was such criminally callous practices that finally enraged sweatshop workers out of their timidity and into the American labor movement. Businesses had an easy

answer for job actions: Call the neighborhood gang leader and rent some thugs to break heads. But eventually, the more prescient mobsters saw a smarter play. If management paid handsomely to end a work stoppage, what might it pay to ensure that a strike never started? To repackage the protection policies sold to

The economic deck was stacked against more than foreigners: New York State dairy workers protested wages.

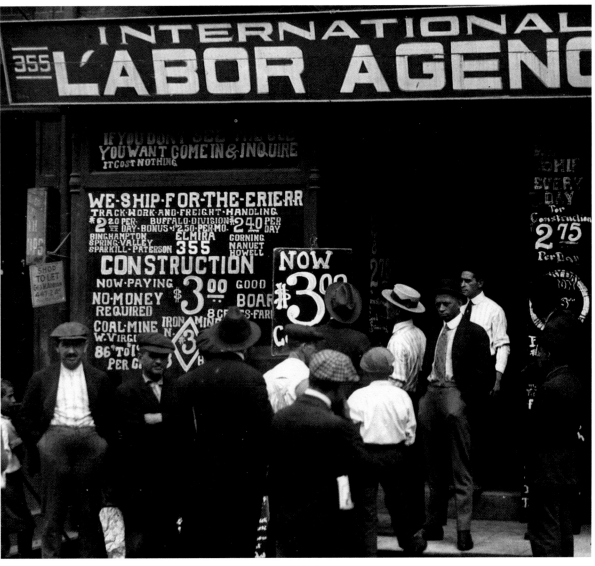

Desperate immigrants looking for jobs took any day work they could find.

Strike

...om-and-pop shops for executive suite ...nsumption, the underworld had to gain ...ntrol of the unions. Ironically, one of the ...rst to fall represented New York's gar...ent workers; by the early 1920s, it was ...ntrolled by a cunning young gangster ...med Arnold Rothstein.

A Buck a Fist

In 1909, these strikebreakers not only had their own headquarters on East 26th Street in Manhattan but could also afford to dress far better than the workers they brutalized. Within a decade, though, men like these had ostensibly switched sides and could be found loitering in union halls.

Highwayman at 17

Burglar at 17

Murderer at 19

Pickpocket at 15

Burglar at 19

Highwayman at 18

Pickpocket at 13

Highwayman at 19

Pit Stop for Mobsters-in-the-Making

In the early 1900s, many New Yorkers knew who to blame for the rapidly rising crime rate. So did the editors of *McClure's* magazine: "From one small spot on the East Side crime arose and spread all over the city—like pestilence from a swamp." That small spot, of course, encompassed the immigrant slums of Manhattan. The popular (and xenophobic) perception was reinforced by the burgeoning population of the Tombs, an infamous prison that received those who broke the law in lower Manhattan, regardless of age or the severity of the crime (above). Just as the graduates of prestigious universities tended to keep in touch later in life, so did alumni of the Tombs. Future leaders of American organized crime served time as youths in that grim building.

HISTORICALLY IN THE *20th century, what we're talking about are ethnic groups that got together committing criminal acts for business purposes to make large amounts of money. In a way, it was their way of breaking into the society. The Protestants, some Catholics, other ethnic groups had already done it. There weren't laws in those days. What they did, what the Jay Goulds did, or the original J. Pierpont Morgan did. Rockefeller. They weren't necessarily caught doing it. Antitrust laws didn't come in until the 1880s and later, so they weren't prosecuted. What they were doing wasn't considered—it might have been unethical and immoral or whatever—but it wasn't necessarily illegal. The areas that were open for these people were vice, gambling, labor unions, certain kinds of industries that were growing in the 20th century, in particular entertainment, leisure, and so on, so they moved into these areas. They developed them, they gave them order, they gave them some kind of structure, and in some cases, they themselves, if they were successful, became legitimate. One good example was Moses Annenberg, who used to run the distribution network for some of the major newspapers before there was television. If you wanted to get your newspaper out, who was going to help you win the newspaper battle would be Moe Annenberg and his army of thugs, who would beat up the newspaper boys.*

—LOWELL BERGMAN
producer, 60 Minutes

And Justice for All—Except the Sons of Italy

By 1890, there were an estimated 30,000 Italian immigrants living in a New Orleans slum known as Little Palermo. Leaders of the community went to the city's police chief, David Hennessey, to complain that a group of Sicilian thugs was extorting tribute. Hennessey agreed to make inquiries. But on a rainy October night, he was ambushed and mortally wounded. The mayor immediately ordered a mass roundup of Italians, 19 of whom were indicted for murder (even though eyewitnesses insisted the gunmen numbered five). When the first six to stand trial (above) were acquitted, a mob of 10,000 stormed their jail, shooting nine prisoners dead and lynching two more. Asked about the vigilanteism, Theodore Roosevelt called it "rather a good thing."

The Myth of the Black Hand

Beginning in the late 19th century, Italian immigrants being extorted by their fellow countrymen often received notes signed only with an inky handprint: the *mano nero*, or black hand. It didn't take America's tabloid journalists long to trumpet that the extortionists were members of a cabal that stretched not only across the ocean whence these "garlic-eating" foreigners came, but also (shiver shiver) back through untold centuries of Old World depredations. In fact, a secret society taking the name Black Hand had arisen in Spain 400 years earlier—to right the wrongs of the Inquisition. Sicilian bandits later found the signature sinister and began using it to petrify their victims.

Don't Stir the Melting Pot

In a spaghetti parlor in turn-of-the-century New York City, Italian immigrants, like many other ethnic groups, banded together to maintain traditions and ethnic identities in the melting pot of urban America.

Why the House Never Loses

By 1900, there were 45 states in the union but gambling was permitted in none (Nevada did not change its law until 1931). Yet illegal dens, like this one, flourished across America because local cops and pols were all too willing to accept grease. Once the graft took root, the pay-offs could only grow as vices like bootleg liquor during Prohibition and, later, drugs yielded higher profits.

PETROSINO IN ITALIAN *means parsley, Number One. When they used to see this cop comin' down the street, they feared him. Really, really did. He was doin' a helluva job combating La Mano Nero, the Black Hand, in that era. So much so that every time a Mafia member from the other side, from Sicily, would come to New York, a fellow member would take him in front of the police headquarters and wait across the street on a corner until he saw Petrosino come out of the building, and he would point with his eyes, he would point, "Questo. Questo qua." That means in English, "This one here." He was the most famous Italian in New York City.*
—WILLIAM BALSAMO
crime historian

The Righteous Serve Up a Bitter Brew:
Prohibition

The notion of temperance, rooted in America's Puritan heritage, took full flower after the turn of the century. Leading the movement were evangelists like Billy Sunday (right), a 19th-century professional baseball pitcher who in retirement found drying out a nation at least as rewarding as striking out a batter. In December 1919, Congress amended the Constitution for the 18th time; when the measure was ratified by the states a scant 13 months later, it became illegal to manufacture, import, distribute or sell alcoholic beverages in the United States. Interestingly, though, the amendment did not ban the purchase or consumption of spirits, setting up this paradox: Law-abiding Americans could drink—if they knew a rumrunner. It was a no-win situation for the nation's law enforcement agencies, a fact finally conceded with the enactment of Repeal in 1933 (two years before the death of Billy Sunday). But the failed social experiment had afforded the criminals who came to dominate bootlegging the opportunity to establish an all but unshakable grip on America.

PROHIBITION WAS A REAL *benefit to the Mob because it provided them with an opportunity to provide a service people wanted. It's impossible to pass laws that are going to control the public morality. When you have twenty million people in the country who want to do drugs, there's no way you're going to pass laws to make it illegal and stop it. The same way with drinking. I mean, it was not possible to stop drinking in this country. So in order for that to exist, in order for all these people to participate in a particular lifestyle, the police in one form or another had to go along. So relationships developed between organized crime and organized police; and these relationships continued to grow over the years. Many policemen became reflections of the people that they policed. They acted like them, talked like them, walked like them.*

— ROBERT LEUCI
author

SED

ATION OF

OHIBITION ACT

DER OF

DISTRICT COURT

RICT OF _____

n to enter premises without
TED STATES MARSHAL

PROHIBITION?
Then Make the
Martini Dry

Although Congress and the states enacted Prohibition, in a democracy the people had the final vote—and as a nation, America continued to imbibe. The hypocrisy of the situation was stunning. While federal revenue agents were padlocking two-bit gin mills and chasing after mountain moonshiners, the well-connected tippled at hoity-toity speakeasies like New York's "21" Club (left). In short order, bootlegging became too lucrative to leave to the small fry. It was during the dark and bloody battles for control of liquor distribution that America's underworld began its evolution from a series of isolated fiefdoms into a union of criminal city-states.

e secret liquor cellar at the "21" Club

WHEN THE PROHIBITION *agents would knock on the door, Jimmy the doorman would press a button. A bell would ring inside the bar, and all the people seated, who were drinking from their demitasse cups, would either gulp it down or throw it down, and the bar had an automatic shelf drop. By pressing a button, everything that was on the shelves, all the bottles from which you poured your whiskey, inverted. The bottles dropped onto a tremendous pile of rocks, and all that was left was the odor. No liquor was found or anything, and they searched in here for about ten hours. My brother Jack had the door [to the liquor cellar] built. The guy who did it was a locksmith who had a shop on Sixth Avenue, and it took about a year to match up every brick, because they had to match the mortar between the bricks. The door is about a foot thick and with a finger you can push it open. It really is a mechanical genius stunt.*
—PETER KRIENDLER
"21" Club

Chapter Two

Changing of the Guard

In May 1925, Angelo Genna, vilest of six brothers who ran Chicago bootlegging, got iced; his funeral was swell. Next to go: Mike. When brother Tony was hit in July, even his moll skipped the services, and surviving siblings Pete, Sam and Jim fled.

Prohibition
Magna Carta for the Mob

THERE WERE MEN OF GENIUS in the history of crime in America, men who would have become bright lights in the legitimate world if they had so desired or if time and circumstance had conspired to lead them into business, law or politics. Arnold Rothstein is the prototype of this genre, which includes Meyer Lansky, Frank Costello, Longy Zwillman, Frankie Yale, Lucky Luciano and Al Capone—to name just the pantheon.

But all these brains rolled into one could not have created a landscape more inviting, more inevitable, for a flourishing system of crime than the combination of do-gooders and Bible Belt messiahs who thought they could put a great, free, raucous republic on dry by passing an amendment to the Constitution. If Prohibition is not the reigning irony of the American Century, the real thing had better hurry up.

Here was a whole country on thirst and nobody to quench it but wiseguys. The gift was so grand, so volcanic, that it seemed to break the Richter scale of the underworld. Money, money everywhere for guys who only yesterday were hustling for small change. No wonder it took years for the wisest among them to begin to stop the carnage among them.

The Roaring Twenties, as depicted in the movies of the '30s, was a lot closer to reality than Hollywood is today on today. Maybe because the people who wrote the screenplays, like Ben Hecht and Charles MacArthur, had spent their salad days as crime reporters in Chicago. Dodge City was nothing next to Chicago in the 1920s, where machine guns took the place of knives and forks as silverware in the town that Billy Sunday could not shut down.

Of course, Chicago was Al Capone, "Scarface" to the world. Capone, in his twenties, ran Chicago like a Roman emperor. "I own the police," he announced, and this was an understatement. To "run" the police you had to control the politicians, and Capone accomplished this by wiping out Deanie O'Banion, the flower-loving Irish gangster. After Deanie died among his roses, Scarface had clear running with Mayor Big Bill Thompson and the Illinois legislature.

"All dictators look good—until the last ten minutes," wrote John Gunther. It fits as Al Capone's epitaph. The event was the St. Valentine's Day Massacre of 1929. Capone sent his gunsels into a Chicago garage to wipe out the remnants of the O'Banion gang. Capone's boys were dressed as cops, and this outraged the media and the country.

More important, it upset the wise men who were making fortunes on Prohibition: Longy Zwillman of Newark, who was bringing in half the packaged goods from Canada, the Meyer and Bug gang who ran New York, the young turks of the Mafia, led by Lucky Luciano. The last thing these men needed was scandal, while the country was happy with its speakeasies where all you had to say was "Gus sent me."

And while the young head of the FBI, J. Edgar Hoover, was telling the country that there was no such thing as organized crime.

Even in Chicago there were influential men who understood that Al Capone had gone a bridge too far. And none more than Moses Annenberg, who began his racketeering life as William Randolph Hearst's circulation man in Chicago and would soon set up the national wire for horse betting.

Annenberg hooked up with Longy Zwillman, the man who set up the Combination, the forerunner of the national syndicate of crime. The Combination was originally all Jewish, from Lansky in New York to the Detroit Purple Gang to the Cleveland mob run by Moe Dalitz.

Zwillman had a tight connection with Capone, the first Italian mobster who didn't care whether his people were born in Sicily or Romania. Capone's organization was called the Outfit, and to get in you just had to know how to shoot straight; religion and birthplace made no matter to Scarface. This was Capone's legacy, and the Outfit still rides high in Chicago.

But Scarface was more of a problem than a friend after St. Valentine's Day. And so came the Atlantic City Convention of 1929.

This meeting, famous in Mafia history, was really dominated by Jews—both to set up the country in an organized fashion and to read the riot act to Al Capone. A few days later, Capone gave himself up on a petty larceny charge in Philadelphia. It would lead to his demise.

And it would lead to the national crime federation, where Jews, Italians, Irish and all creeds and colors would live together—until death, or the feds, did them part. ★

The Melting Pot Thickens

By World War I, the Irish gangs that ruled the vices were facing competition from innovative Jewish and Italian hoodlums. Gambler Arnold Rothstein (above) gained notoriety for fixing the 1919 Black Sox World Series; less visible was his tutoring of up-and-comers like Meyer Lansky and Lucky Luciano in setting up efficient organizations. Abner (Longy) Zwillman (middle left) sewed up the New Jersey rackets so tightly that he remained a state power until 1959, when at 60 he allegedly garroted himself to death. Moses Annenberg (left), who founded a national sports wire to service bookmakers, pleaded guilty to tax evasion and did three years in the Big House to spare his only boy from a possible conviction for tax evasion. Son Walter became a publishing mogul, Nixon buddy and U.S. ambassador. Big Jim Colosimo (top left) ran a Chicago café, but his meal ticket was a stable of brothels. Brilliantly managing the houses was a nephew from New York, Johnny Torrio (in fedora, center), who in 1919 imported to the Windy City an enforcer from home: Al Capone, then 20.

THE SENIOR FIVE POINTS *gang boss was Paul Kelly. But his real name was Paulo Vacarelli. He was Italian. He looked more like a banker than a hoodlum. He was one prominent member. Also in the gang were Salvatore Lucania, alias Charles (Lucky) Luciano, Alfonse Capone, and most colorful, a man by the name of Francesco Yoelle, alias Frankie Yale, who was the first celebrity Godfather of New York City. No question about it. Yale was sorta like an Italian Robin Hood. He would rob from the rich and give to the poor. The Five Points gang also included other ethnic groups, like you had some Jewish gangsters who belonged to it. Irish gangsters belonged. Yale was so beloved by a lot of people that they called him the Prince of Pals, because of his kindness toward the poor. He really did a lot for the poor through the '20s. He also tutored Al Capone. Capone served his apprenticeship in organized crime at the knee of Frankie Yale.*

—WILLIAM BALSAMO
crime historian

His Last Boola-Boola

For thirsting after bootleg booze that belonged to Al Capone, Brooklyn rackets king Frankie Yale was treated to an early last call. Even though he was no Ivy League genius, Yale, 43, should've seen it coming. He and Capone went back a long way, to the Five Points gang of the 1910s. Later, he had traveled west a couple of times to personally rid Al of two rivals (Big Jim Colosimo and Deanie O'Banion). But Yale could not keep his mitts off Capone's merchandise, so in 1928 he became the first New Yorker slain by that signature Chicago gat, the machine gun. Some 10,000 spectators turned out to see his funeral procession, a $50,000 extravaganza featuring 38 carloads of flowers. Among the mourners: Two women with papers that said she was Mrs. Yale.

The Mob's Favorite Fed

In 1917, 22-year-old J. Edgar Hoover joined the U.S. Department of Justice and began a crime-fighting career that was to span more than half a century. In 1924 he was appointed director of the department's then ill-regarded Bureau of Investigation (which became the FBI in 1935), and served as the nation's top G-man until his death in 1972. Hoover spent the Depression glorifying his agency (not to mention himself) by hotly pursuing and sometimes collaring adolescent car thieves and two-bit criminals like Machine Gun Kelly, Ma Barker, Pretty Boy Floyd and John Dillinger, whom he labeled "Public Enemies." As for organized crime, Hoover steadfastly denied the very existence of the Mob. Perhaps the image-conscious FBI chief feared his agents were powerless against the strengthening underworld syndicates; perhaps, as recently suggested, the gangsters owned damning evidence about the top cop's private affairs. Or perhaps Hoover simply had a taste for mob-related activities: J. Edgar liked to play the horses. Only in 1957, when state troopers raided an underworld conference in Apalachin, New York, and reeled in some 60 notorious mob figures, was Hoover finally forced to publicly acknowledge organized crime.

RAID!

It's Really No Big Deal

Gambling was a steady source of income for organized crime and raids like this (above) were few and far between, thanks to payoffs to greedy cops and politicians. During Prohibition speakeasies and bootlegging flourished and mob coffers overflowed with profits from illegal booze. With the repeal of the 18th Amendment in 1933, the underworld instinctively switched its focus to other illegal goods and services: gambling, prostitution and drugs. More and more legitimate storefronts became masks for illegal gambling dens despite the complaints of moralists and do-gooders. Some pundits even argued gambling was vital to the nation's health. As former Oklahoma State Representative John Monks put it: "In every country the Communists have taken over, the first thing they do is outlaw cockfighting."

Tools of the Trade

Samuel Colt's .45 (far left) was popular with gangsters nationwide but their weapon of choice was undoubtedly the Thompson submachine gun (near left), affectionately called the tommy gun. Named after its co-inventor, Brigadier General John T. Thompson, and designed for military use, the tommy gun was too expensive and used too much ammunition to satisfy the Army when it first appeared in the 1920s. Organized crime, needless to say, loved it. The tommy gun wasn't even illegal, since existing state and city gun-control laws covered only concealed weapons. After two decades of mob-financed testing, the U.S. military finally came around and bought nearly two million tommy guns during World War II.

Mouthpiece

Lawyer William J. Fallon (seated), the favorite legal eagle of a long string of mobsters, holds a press conference for one of his more reputable clients, former New York Giants outfielder Albert (Cozy) Dolan. Dolan was accused of trying to bribe Philadelphia Nationals shortstop John (Heine) Sand during the 1924 baseball season.

After Sing Sing, He Went Home

Well-connected New York thugs weren't supposed to pull hard time. But in 1913, Owen (Owney) Madden (near right), then a young English goon from Leeds, left live witnesses behind when he waxed a rival—and paid for that carelessness with eight years up the river. Upon his parole, he wisely sought less risky rackets like operating Prohibition-era speakeasies (including Harlem's famed Cotton Club); rum-running; and owning boxers like heavyweight Primo Carnera. But Owney couldn't stay clean; he was sent back to the pen for violating parole. On emerging from Sing Sing in 1933, Madden, by then 41, took stock and decided the time had come to quit Manhattan.

A Family That Owney Had Eyes for Madden

The first Mrs. Madden—Dorothy, with their daughter Marjorie in 1930—had waited for their breadwinner through his various incarcerations. But when Owney moved himself down to Hot Springs, Arkansas, they were not welcome to come. Down in Dixie, it didn't take Madden long to buy off the local bubbas. He took a house next to the chief of police, set up casinos and got hitched a second time (to the postmaster's daughter). But auld acquaintances were not forgot; guests at chez Madden included Lucky Luciano, Bugsy Siegel and New Orleans boss Carlos Marcello.

ORGANIZED CRIME
means you are connected to politics, that's what makes it organized. It's not just because you
have a gang. There are a lot of
gangs of people around, but they
have no other connections.
Organized crime means contacts
with legislators, with DAs, with
judges, with people who can
make sure nothing really bad
happens. That's what makes it
organized. Otherwise it's just
street gangs. There are all these
tentacles—connections with
legitimate business. The money
that flows in is protected by
great tax lawyers. You got corpo-
rations to keep your names out.
Organized crime is a dangerous
thing because it corrupts government, and the public gets badly
hurt, because you're not being
represented by the people you
think are representing you. Was
Moses Annenberg part of organized crime? Was Joseph Kennedy
part of organized crime? Was the
Ford Motor Company part of
organized crime because in the
1930s they retained mobster Joe
Adonis and the Genovese crime
family to protect their trucks
when they delivered cars to New
Jersey from Detroit? Or are they
just "associated" with them?
—SIDNEY ZION
author

BIG BILL

William Hale (Big Bill) Thompson (right)
was a colorful Republican machine leader
who served three terms as mayor of
Chicago (1915-23; 1927-31). He also was
probably the most corrupt politician the
nation has ever seen. When he first took
office Big Bill was backed by such notable
Chicago gangsters as Big Jim Colosimo
(later assassinated on Al Capone's orders)
and Colosimo's nephew Johnny Torrio, and
Diamond Joe Esposito. By his third term he
was Al Capone's personal mayor. Big Bill is
remembered for his rabid anti-British senti-
ments and the Republican primary he led in
Chicago in 1928, known as the Pineapple
Primary. The pineapples were the numerous
bombs thrown by opposing mob factions
during the campaign.

BEAU JAMES
The Big Apple's Lovable Worm

In 1923, a New York State legislator named James John Walker (above center, when he was mayor of New York) defended two-bit hood Louis Kushner, who had been arrested for the murder of mobster Nathan Kaplan, better known as Kid Dropper. A Tammany Hall Democrat, Walker got the charge reduced to manslaughter and saved Kushner from the jolt of the electric chair. Three years later the corrupt but immensely popular Walker, known affectionately as Gentleman Jimmy or Dandy Jim for his flamboyant style, became mayor of New York, to the delight of such notable gangsters as Frank Costello and Lucky Luciano. Chicago, it seems, was to have nothing on the Big Apple. When told that New York City cops needed a raise, debonair Gentleman Jimmy, later portrayed on the silver screen by Bob Hope, responded: "Ah, we can't give 'em one this year. Tell 'em to earn it out on the streets," an incentive program that put New York cops on equal footing with the city's politicians. Mounting corruption charges forced Walker to resign in 1932 before the end of his second term, but the Mob was hardly inconvenienced. Another Tammany Hall hack, John P. O'Brien, took Dandy Jim's place. Finally, in 1933, Fiorello LaGuardia was elected mayor, and the city settled down to an extended run of fairly honest government.

DON'T GET THE IDEA that I'm one of those goddamn radicals. My rackets are run along strict American lines. This American system of ours —call it capitalism, call it what you like—gives each and every one of us a great opportunity, if we only seize it with both hands and make the most of it. I make my money by supplying a public demand. If I break the law, my customers are as guilty as I am. I call myself a businessman. ★

— AL CAPONE

At age 30, the saturnine mug of 220-lb. Alphonse Capone was as familiar to the citizens of Chicago as it was to the city's cops.

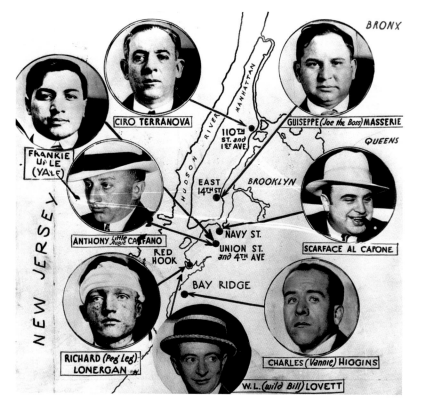

Hat $20.00
Collar $2.00
Necktie $4.95
Shirt $27.50 with Monogram $1.00
Belt Buckle $275.00
Suit $135.00
Silk Underwear $10.00
Overcoat $150.00
Shoes $20.00
Socks $2.00

From Rags to Riches to a Town of His Own

Al Capone was a homegrown talent, born, to be exact, in 1899 in a section of Brooklyn (above) that spawned thugs the way Wisconsin produces cheese. The barber's son learned to shave corners early, joining a youth gang affiliated with the notorious Five Points mob. Other members: Lucky Luciano and Frankie Yale. Capone caught the attention of Johnny Torrio, a Five Points veteran 17 years his senior. Torrio was soon to head west, but he didn't forget his protégé. In 1919, Al was feeling heat over a murder and Johnny needed a hitter. Neither man—nor the city of Chicago—would ever be the same.

A Starter Home for a Family-Minded Man

When Capone was still a minor mobster in New York, he and wife Mae raised their only child, Alphonse Jr., in a brick row house at 38 Garfield Place, Brooklyn. The supportive Mae rarely asked questions about her husband's occupation, and made the spur-of-the-moment move to the Midwest with the alacrity of a corporate wife.

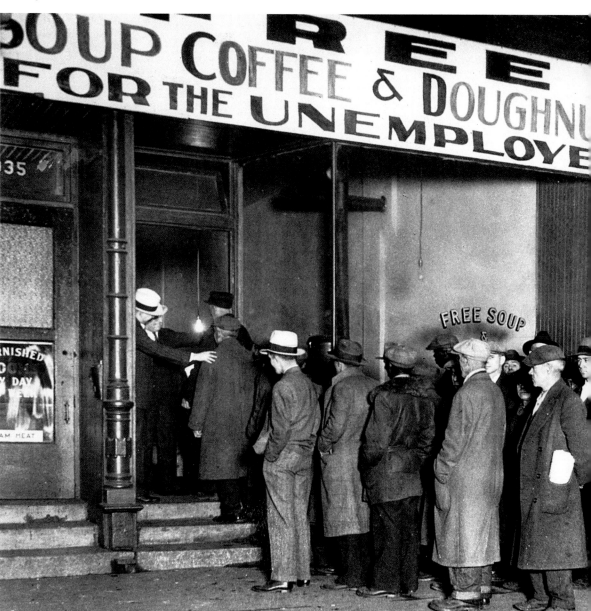

Smile When You Say "Scarface," Stranger

Just 11 years after he landed on Chicago's South Side, Capone had wreaked enough mayhem to land on the cover of *Time*. The magazine reported on his vice industries, as well as his penchant for grandstand ploys, such as shelling out $350 a day to support a Depression-era soup kitchen (below left). The editors allowed themselves to make sport of Capone's lavish threads (diagram, left) and to take the liberty of openly calling him Scarface. The gangster was notoriously touchy about the broad gash across his left cheek, claiming it was an old World War I wound (more likely it had been inflicted by a Sicilian gangster). Capone's willingness to grant *Time* an interview was a sign of a self-confidence that bordered on—and sometimes crossed over into—megalomania. Not only was he unforgiving to enemies real and imagined, but he also controlled his 1,000-thug gang with an iron fist. Though safe in the city whose officials he virtually owned, Capone was hounded for years by the feds both in Chicago (in the person of T-man Eliot Ness) and in his Florida hideaway (by agents in 1930, bottom right). What brought him down, of course, were the bean counters. Capone never paid taxes on his swag, estimated at $20 million a year. By the time the feds obtained his books and charged him with tax evasion in 1929 (above right), he was clearly apprehensive. Rightly so: Capone was convicted and, after a stint in an Atlanta pen, transferred to Alcatraz (right).

A Hell of a Greeting Card

Capone showed his black heart on St. Valentine's Day, 1929, by making a cold-blooded play for the only part of Chicago still not under his thumb. At his behest, an out-of-town mobster offered George (Bugs) Moran, 36, boss of the North Side, a truckload of bootleg. Hurrying to the drop, Moran saw uniformed officers raiding his headquarters at 2122 North Clark Street and quickly took a powder. He was lucky: The cops were in fact Capone hit men who, once inside the garage, tommy-gunned to death six Moran henchmen and a hapless gofer. So corrupt was the police force that Chicagoans first thought the massacre a shakedown gone bad. When the truth emerged, Capone, now 30, was finally seen as not a romantic underworld czar but a mad dog.

Retribution: A Nemesis Named Ness

In 1928, Eliot Ness (right) began to assemble a team of nine special Prohibition agents from the ranks of the Chicago police department. Handpicked for their honesty and determination, Ness's band was dubbed the Untouchables by the Mob because it was unable to either bribe or frighten them. For six years Ness's crew frequently raided Al Capone's distilleries, breweries and warehouses, costing the mob boss a considerable fortune. Capone and Ness never met. After the repeal of Prohibition, Ness moved on to Cleveland where, as public safety director, he successfully took on syndicate boss Moe Dalitz and the Mayfield Road mob.

ONE NIGHT WE ALL WENT *out to a restaurant. Ben [Siegel] protected me all the time. We went into an Italian restaurant in New York. Lepke was there; he was trying to keep from getting executed or something. And we all were having a farewell dinner which we hoped wouldn't be a farewell dinner. And at the Italian restaurant we had a big table spread out, and there was windows, big windows there. And all of a sudden a car comes around and starts machine-gunning the window and Ben yells, "Down!" There was a ladies' room in back of us. I started slithering on my tummy, and there was a space above the ladies' room where the entrance was, and I went in and I stood up on the seats so nobody could see my feet, and I just stayed there. I did what Ben told me. I saw Ben and the boys tip up the table for protection and duck. In a little while Moe came to the door and he said, "Honey, you can come out now." So I came out and I didn't know what I was gonna find because most of the wives and sweethearts who were there were heavier than I was. Some of them were big, and they couldn't have crawled like me! Anyway, the table was all set again with new antipasti, and nothing was ever mentioned. That was it.*

—BEATRICE SEDWAY
*widow of Moe Sedway,
Bugsy Siegel associate*

Phil D'Andrea (left), Al Capone's man Friday, is lead into Chicago's Federal Building by a marshal.

ead poisoning at a New Jersey restaurant

WHEN MY GRANDFATHER *was alive, crime was organized. There were no hoods or kids who smashed windows or stole pocketbooks, that was unheard of. Maybe they stole a piece of fruit, but they didn't hurt anybody. They only hurt people they knew. They didn't hit some woman who was traveling from Germany to Disney World. They were different kind of men. They had their code of honor. They knew exactly what to do. They weren't into drugs. They had to do what they had to do to survive. As far as I'm concerned, my grandfather wasn't bad like some of these kids who just killed a foreigner on a vacation for no good reason. I mean, he killed for a reason. He killed somebody that bothered him or did something to him. Not a stranger, you know? Straight legitimate people want to know about the Mob because it was untouchable. They were untouchable. And I was related to them. Being related worked for me. Anytime I would go out with somebody, and it wasn't working, I just told them who I was, and you would see an instant change in their personality. I mean, they were so nice to me. They were like my best friend. If I couldn't get a job or something like that, if I ever hinted who my father was, and if that didn't work, who my grandfather was, I had the job the next day. Regardless of whether I could spell or I could read, they gave me the job. How long I kept the job was another story. But it worked. It worked.*

—DORIE SHAPIRO
GRIZZARD
Gurrah Shapiro's granddaughter

Get a Grip on It

Seemingly unbridled violence and corruption led first to frustration and then to public outrage, as evidenced by this cartoon from the heyday of the Mob. Organized crime was infiltrating every level of American society, despite promises by obviously inept law enforcement agencies. Gangsters were literally getting away with murder, and it appeared that no one could stop them, not even the long arm of the law. Something had to be done.

82 Chair Parade at Night, Atlantic City, N. J.

7A-H3504

By the Sea, By the Sea

In 1929, while law-abiding citizens enjoyed the many pleasures of the Atlantic City boardwalk, under their unsuspecting noses the seaside resort's mob boss, Nucky Johnson, hosted an important conference of the nation's leading gangsters. Convened by Meyer Lansky and Johnny Torrio, the meeting, thought to be the first of its kind, ultimately led to the dissolution of the old-style Mob and its replacement by a new and ethnically varied organized crime network of national proportions.

A Dip in the River

ops and other law enforcement officers examine the
emains of mob victims fished out of New York's East River
the summer of 1935. Grisly scenes like this one were all
oo common in the nation's cities, even after the repeal of
rohibition. Organized crime somehow continued to flourish,
nd an enraged public began to cry out for retribution and
eform.

I Will Always Love Al

Mae Coughlan, who on December 18, 1918, became Mrs. Al Capone, remained so devoted to the fallen gangster that she even braved photographers to visit him on the Rock in 1938. But her trips west to Alcatraz soon ended. Because Capone was afraid of needles, he had never sought treatment for the syphilis contracted from a long-ago dalliance; by the late '30s, the disease had reduced him to a drooling vegetable. In 1939, he was certified insane and released to Mae, who took him to their Florida estate. There he continued barking out orders to his lackeys—only now, no one bothered to jump. Capone died in 1947, at 48. After burying him in Chicago, Mae loyally spurned a $50,000 offer to write her autobiography; she died in 1988.

No New Deal for the Old Guard

On April 15, 1931, Sicilian butcher Giuseppe (Joe the Boss) Masseria, 51, had just drawn an ace when he was trumped by Luciano gunsels at a Coney Island restaurant. Five months later, Salvatore Maranzano, at 63 the last of the Sicilian overlords, was shot and stabbed to death in his Manhattan office by four men flashing badges. The next generation of gangsters—perhaps no more vicious, but certainly smarter, more visionary and greedier—was loudly making its entrance from the wings.

Chapter Three
Conquer and Divide

The gunmen who rubbed out Chicago gangster Johnny Genero in 1931 were unerring shots—his bodyguard, Jimmy Vince, emerged without a scratch. True to the underworld code, Jimmy didn't see nothin'.

The Thirties
What Depression?

THE 1930S ARE KNOWN AS America's hangover, the long black nightmare that followed the big binge of the Roaring Twenties. For the mobs of America, however, the '20s were an hors d'oeuvre, the '30s their T-bone steak.

No gangster ever jumped out of a Wall Street window; to the contrary, the wise men of the Combination and the shrewd young turks of the Mafia viewed the stock market crash as a great new gift from the Promised Land. They strode into the new decade laden with cash, just when cash was king as never before.

Cash could get you choice real estate parcels at dirt prices and major shares in companies that were starving but would turn into cash cows in the future. Most important, cash got you together with the party bosses and the elected politicians and judges they controlled like so many puppets on a string.

The men who met in Atlantic City in the spring of 1929 did not foresee October's Black Monday or they would have sold short and retired. They did know that Prohibition was terminal and that a national cartel was as necessary to them as it had been to the robber barons. They also knew that a cartel would not happen without bloodshed.

In 1931, the crucial decision was made— the Mafia would have to be brought into the 20th century. Lucky Luciano was the ticket. He had long been champing at the bit against the reactionary Mustache Petes, Joe (the Boss) Masseria and Salvatore Maranzano. His boyhood pals Meyer Lansky and Bugsy Siegel promoted the idea with the Combination that, in the name of national unity, Masseria and Maranzano had to go.

And it was done. The Combination took in the Italians, who now began to run the Mafia on a business basis—the American Mafia, no longer the Italian Mafia.

The Combination was ready for the post-Prohibition world. Lepke Buchalter and Gurrah Shapiro had pioneered industrial rackets in New York's garment center. Working both sides of the street, labor and the bosses, Lepke and Gurrah cornered the industry in a brilliant criminal stroke that bred the Teamsters Union. Fifty trucks distributed clothing to America, and all they had was a company union. Break a few heads and what have you got? Control over the garment industry. If you want to ship, you come to Lepke and Gurrah.

At the 1932 Democratic Convention in Chicago, the crime cartel showed its national muscle by laying their money and boss connections in for Franklin D. Roosevelt. Jimmy Hines, the Tammany leader on Dutch Schultz's Harlem numbers pad, shared a room with Luciano at the Hotel Drake, while Lepke wined and dined the downtown bosses. FDR showed his appreciation by leaving the bosses alone on their turf, which meant that the Mob could run its rackets without federal interference.

But a wave of reform was on New York, following disclosures that wrecked the career of Jimmy Walker, the night mayor. Fiorello LaGuardia rode into City Hall and immediately fanned the flames against the Mob. A Republican Wall Street lawyer named Thomas E. Dewey was named special prosecutor and nearly rode his racket-busting grand juries to the White House.

Dewey put away a bunch of big names—Luciano, Lepke, Gurrah Shapiro, Waxey Gordon and Jimmy Hines—but he didn't put a dent in the cartel. Dutch Schultz was his earliest target, and this so infuriated the "crazy Dutchman" that he put out a contract on Dewey—against the express veto of the Combination. The wise men had Schultz killed instead.

As the decade came to a close, Dewey—who had already convicted Luciano of running a prostitution ring—now named Lepke Buchalter the Public Enemy Number One. Lepke went into hiding, while sending Abe (Kid Twist) Reles and his gang of Brooklyn hit men out to eradicate anybody who might possibly know enough to turn state's evidence on Lep.

The tabloids dubbed the gang Murder Inc., and with that sobriquet sold more newspapers than there were people to kill.

But the Combination shook all of this trouble off and carried on full steam ahead. Ben Siegel took over Los Angeles from the Mustache Petes and put a nice stranglehold on the movie industry. The Hollywood moguls and stars loved Siegel, whom they never called Bugsy. George Raft dressed like him, and it got so that you couldn't tell whether the mob guys were emulating the movie stars or vice versa.

But if vice got top billing, who cared? ★

Legends in Their Own Minds

During the 1930s, Midnight Rose's, a Brooklyn candy store, served as the office of Murder Inc., the national crime syndicate's enforcement arm, thought to be responsible for perhaps 500 murders over the course of the decade. Three of the enforcers who regularly frequented the candy store were (above, left to right) Pittsburgh Phil Strauss, Happy Maione, and Frank (the Dasher) Abbandando. Strauss was Murder Inc.'s heaviest hitter, thought to be responsible for 100 killings; Abbandando ran a respectable second with about 50. All three ended up in the electric chair. The guiding principle of Murder Inc. was enunciated by Bugsy Siegel: "We only killed our own." That rule was tested in 1935 when Dutch Schultz demanded a contract be put out on New York special prosecutor Thomas E. Dewey (right). Dewey, who later served three terms as governor of New York, twice ran unsuccessfully for president. He was largely responsible for sending Lucky Luciano and other mobsters to prison, and cracking down on Schultz's rackets. The syndicate's governing board rejected Dutch's call for Dewey's murder and promptly had Schultz himself rubbed out. Murder Inc. was dismantled in the early 1940s, thanks to the testimony of small-time hit man Kid Twist Reles, "the canary of Murder Inc."

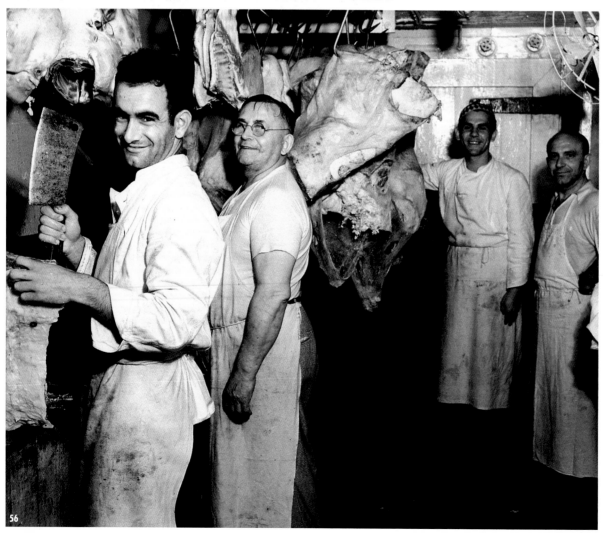

Muscling into the Legit World

Just one generation earlier, the U.S. labor movement had gotten a powerful lift when pioneer muckrackers like Jacob Riis, Ida Tarbell and Frank Norris published exposés on how Big Business exploited its workers. But by the 1930s, many American unions had been brutally intimidated into accepting a silent partner: the Mob. In New York City alone, various syndicates ruled the unions for construction (above, workers erecting the Empire State Building); the garment industry (top left); fishmongering (middle left); and meatpacking (left). Not only were many workers forced to pay kickbacks to land a job, but control of the unions was also a stepping-stone to more profits, for it allowed gangsters to use the threat of a strike to shake down management.

23-Skidoo!
Despite Depression, the Rackets Rocketed

One out of four Americans may have been jobless, but the 75 percent with money in their pockets made vice one of America's few growth industries. A society that tolerated illegal speakeasies—by one estimate, 200,000 nationwide and 32,000 in New York City alone—wasn't about to deny itself a few friendly hands of cards, the den at bottom had a hot line to the nearest precinct (in case rivals came raiding). To be sure, cops across the land launched photogenic crackdowns against bootleggers, gamblers and the ladies who practiced the second oldest profession. But these were rightly seen by the Mob enterprises as mere nuisances, one of the costs of doing business.

Mining for Mobsters

Tipped that a couple of hoods had been buried by their Murder Inc. killers in a Lyndhurst, New Jersey, backyard, local cops broke out the shovels. It was a drill they knew well; over two decades, the elite mob enforcers were thought to have carried out as many as 500 executions. The Brooklyn-based organization took great pains to rub out only their underworld brethren. The pay (up to $5,000 per hit) and fringe benefits (like pensions) were excellent, but in truth, the psychopaths who sought a place on the Murder Inc. payroll would most likely have killed for nothing.

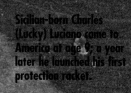

Sicilian-born Charles (Lucky) Luciano came to America at age 9; a year later he launched his first protection racket.

Murder Inc. was famous for making its contracts—even on a busy New York street in broad daylight.

LATER I FOUND OUT, that is, the girls told me. "Don't you know who you're sitting with? You're sitting with Murder Incorporated guys and Mafia!" And I said,"What's Murder Incorporated? And what's Mafia?" Oh, well, geepers, every time there was something in the paper, they would show me it. And I said, "You have to be wrong, because this fellow that's taking me out is so nice and so quiet and so sweet. He's shy, he never puts a finger on me." Every night I was getting—like all the other girls—beautiful flowers, and they'd have a diamond bracelet in them, and on the third date he had a big diamond on his pinkie, which was the only piece of jewelry I wore for the rest of my life.

—BEATRICE SEDWAY
widow of Moe Sedway
Bugsy Siegel associate

PEOPLE BELIEVE THAT *anybody could've went to Murder Inc. and had their husband assassinated, their wife or their rich uncle. Not so. They were only available as killers to the underworld. Nationally, any gang in the nation that had any power could use their services. Let's say the gang came from Cleveland. They would have to retain them and maybe pay like $25,000 annually to retain them plus a fee for each victim. Some of your top killers were Pittsburgh Phil Strauss, Emmanuel Mindy Weiss, Abe Reles, of course, Frank (the Dasher) Abbandando, Happy Maione and another guy, Charlie (the Bug) Workman, who helped wipe out the Dutch Schultz mob.*

— WILLIAM BALSAMO
crime historian

THIS IS OUR LIFE. *This is how things are in the Cosa Nostra. It could be our brother, but if someone does something wrong, he has to pay the penalty. And Nicky said, "When you shoot somebody, you don't shoot him from a mile away. You gotta walk right up and put the gun right behind his head and shoot him. And you always shoot 'em in the head. You never want any mistakes; you want to shoot 'em in the head, and then if you want, shoot him in the chest, but you gotta make sure at least a couple bullets get in the head."*

— PHILIP LEONETTI
ex-Philadelphia underboss

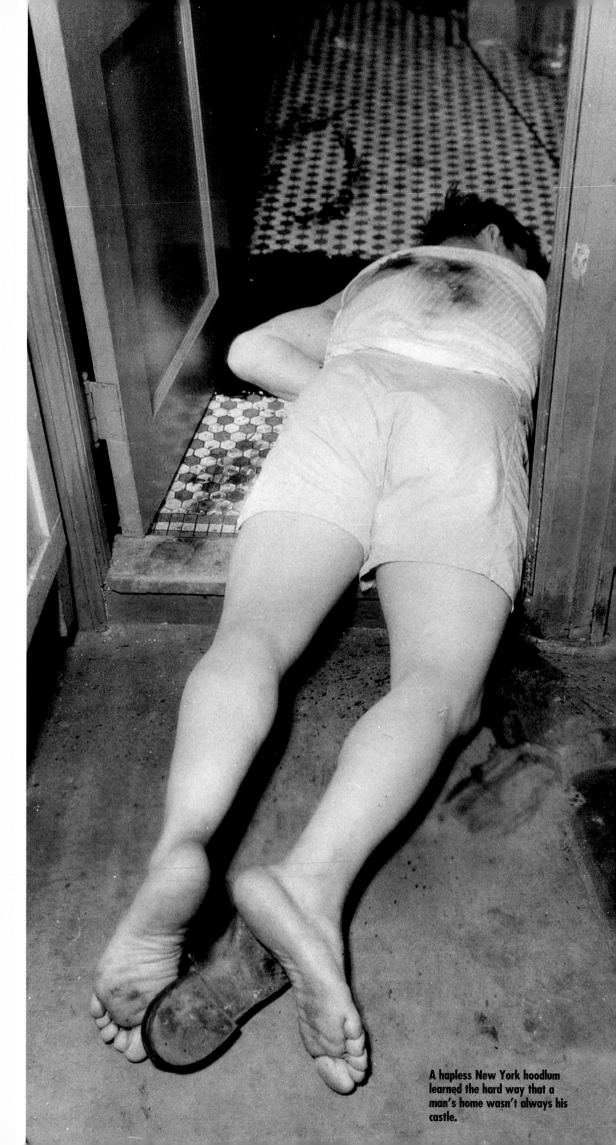

A hapless New York hoodlum learned the hard way that a man's home wasn't always his castle.

In America, diminutive Polish-born Maier Suchowljansky became Meyer Lansky, the Jewish brainiac of organized crime.

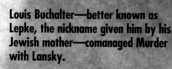
Louis Buchalter—better known as Lepke, the nickname given him by his Jewish mother—comanaged Murder with Lansky.

Like Houdini, this underworld tough ended up in a trunk; unlike the escape artist, he didn't emerge alive.

WHEN LEPKE'S FATHER *died, he was a fish peddler on the Lower East Side. His mother moved out to Denver, where his brother later became the chief rabbi. Lepke was put to live with his sister, who had just gotten married, and he didn't like it. He didn't like the whole setup, and that is when he went out on the street with this A average, and he started to push over push-carts and steal money off the streets, and he became a major criminal. You wonder what would have happened if that did-n't happen. He was the only one in his family who was a criminal. It was a very respectable family. You see this a lot in the Jewish families. One guy is the black sheep, usually it's the younger one, and the others are legitimate.*
—SIDNEY ZION
author

THE BUSINESS ABOUT *mobsters caring about their immediate families, I think it's important to them to rationalize their own behavior. So if they sat in a car and blew the brains out of some guy, and then immedi-ately went home to a Christmas party or a christening and hugged and kissed their children, held their children on their laps, when somebody whose head they just blew off in a car is no longer going to go home or have any kids sitting on their laps—they have to rationalize that. They look in the mirror and they say, "This is me, and I'm not an evil person. I love this child. I'll take care of this child, and if anyone talks badly about you, I'll kill them because I'm your friend."*
—ROBERT LEUCI
author

THEY WERE EVIL PEOPLE. *And I stuck it in my mind, even as far as God's concerned, that I'm not doing anything wrong. I'm killing somebody who is an evil person, someone even the government's looking to indict or give the electric chair to. I'm not killing a person who's a good citizen, someone who's a doctor helping people. We're not crazed killers, at least I didn't think we were at the time. We wouldn't go out and kill little kids. We would kill people that disrespected our family, and I thought that was good. We were respectable people. We'd help other Italian people if we could. The Black Hand would come in and shake their own kind down. But we got rid of the Black Hand and the Mafia. We didn't want to suck blood from our own kind. We were there to help people. But as things start evolving and changing and people started dealing with drugs, it's not like it was in the old days.*

—PHILIP LEONETTI
ex-Philadelphia underboss

IT WAS MY WIFE'S BIRTH-*day, and we were all at the party. Roy came over, and he said, "Guess who's on the corner on 85th Street? Vinnie Mook." I had to tell my wife we were leaving the birthday party. We all got disguises and we went and shot him in the street. Then we went over the Brooklyn Bridge and gave all our clothes away to the bums and went back to the party like nothing happened. We had cake and handed out the presents.*

—DOMINICK MONTIGLIO
former Gambino family associate

New York City's
police photographers,
collecting evidence,
snapped the Murder
Inc.'s stiffs.

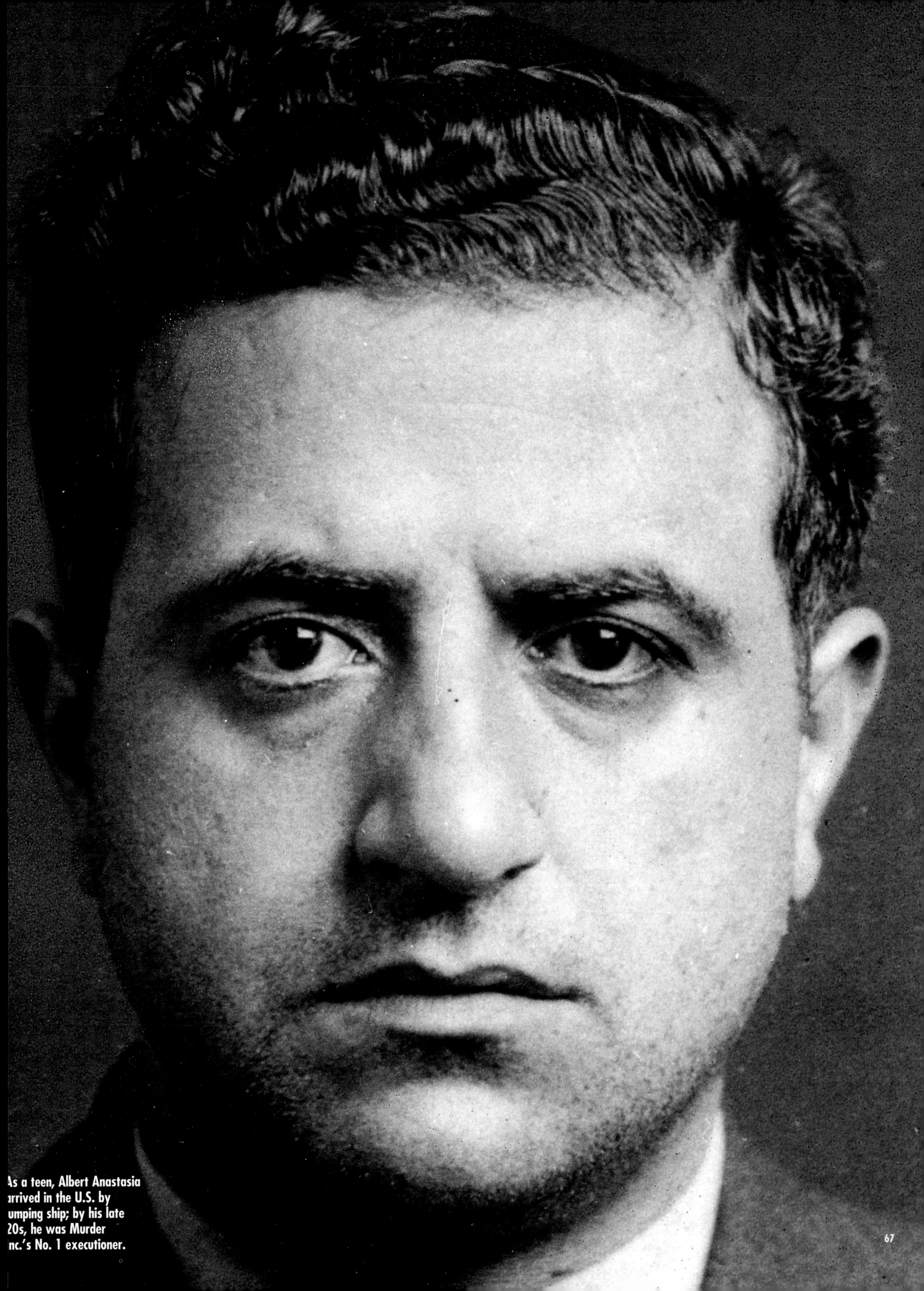

As a teen, Albert Anastasia
arrived in the U.S. by
jumping ship; by his late
20s, he was Murder
Inc.'s No. 1 executioner.

When Irish Eyes Could Still Smile

In 1938, New York Democratic rainmaker Jimmy Hines (left) was charged with being in cahoots with mobster Dutch Schultz, but seemed confident of beating the rap. He did. But the next spring, at age 62, Hines was retried, convicted on 13 counts and sent up the river to Sing Sing, where he tended the inmates' garden for four years.

Flower Power!

Fiorello LaGuardia, 52, got his first term as mayor of New York City off to a smashing start in 1934 by sledgehammering confiscated slot machines into scrap. The pudgy politician, nicknamed the Little Flower, was voted in at the head of a fusion ticket that vowed to weed out corruption. But despite LaGuardia's sincere efforts—his personal integrity was never questioned—the city remained a hothouse in which organized crime flourished throughout the Depression. Indeed, the chief legacies of LaGuardia's three terms in office were his radio show, on which he read comics to kids whose parents were too broke to afford a newspaper, and the airport in Queens that bears his name.

California Dreaming

A 1940 free-for-all in a San Francisco shipyard, instigated by a mob-run sailors' union, served public notice that organized crime had branched westward. Down the coast, Hollywood moguls were paying out millions to Willie Bioff and George Browne, two Chicago hoods who had taken over a Midwestern stagehands union. The studios, though, received useful services for their money.

I HEARD ABOUT THIS *furniture factory. I was a smart kid, so I go to the furniture factory and I says, "Who's the boss?" and I start talking to him. I says, "How's the chances of me goin' into the factory and shylocking?" And he says, "I don't want no gangstahs in my place." I didn't give up. There was a union organizer, so I got a hold of him and I says, "How would you like to make a couple of hundred dollars?" He says, "Doing what?" I says, "Pull the factory out on a strike." So he says, "That's all I got to do?" I says, "Yeah." He pulls the factory and they go on a strike. So I go to the boss. I say, "Hey, I could fix that for you. If I get them to take the strike off, would you let me in the factory?" He says, "Sure!" I go up to Shotgut and I says, "Shotgut, here's your two hundred dollars. Call off the strike." The strike is called off. Now I'm in the factory, so I says, "How does these guys get paid?" There was about 150 men working in the factory. He says, "I pay 'em by check every Friday." I says, "Could you hold it off until the afternoon?" He says, "Sure." I says, "What's the payroll?" Let's say it was three, four thousand dollars. I says, "You give me the three thousand dollars, and I'll sit in the office and let them come to me and cash their checks. The bank will be closed, and I'll charge each man a dollar to cash their checks." He says, "That's nothing." So that's what he did. He paid them after the banks closed, and I used to get the money and I cashed their checks. It was a good racket.*

—PHIL WEISS
former racketeer

One Dead Dutchman

The same temper that landed this New York tough on his deathbed was the key to his rapid rise in the underworld. During World War I, teenager Arthur Flegenheimer renamed himself Dutch Schultz. A decade later, using booty from several heists, Dutch bought two saloons. It took him a homicidal decade to build bootlegging, numbers and the slots into a multimillion-dollar-a-year empire. But while Schultz was preoccupied fighting a tax-evasion charge, Lucky Luciano, Meyer Lansky and Longy Zwillman began muscling into his rackets. Rather than fight, Dutch expanded into New Jersey and accepted a high role in the infant syndicate. The truce was broken when Manhattan D.A. Tom Dewey went after the slot machines that Schultz still controlled. The infuriated gangster swore he would personally kill the prosecutor; the Mob, fearing the fallout from such a hit, called in Murder Inc. On October 23, 1935, Charles (the Bug) Workman strode into a Newark chophouse and ventilated the 33-year-old Schultz with hot lead. Tough to the end, the victim hung on for two days, ranting non sequiturs. His last words: "French-Canadian bean soup. I want to pay. Let me leave them alone!"

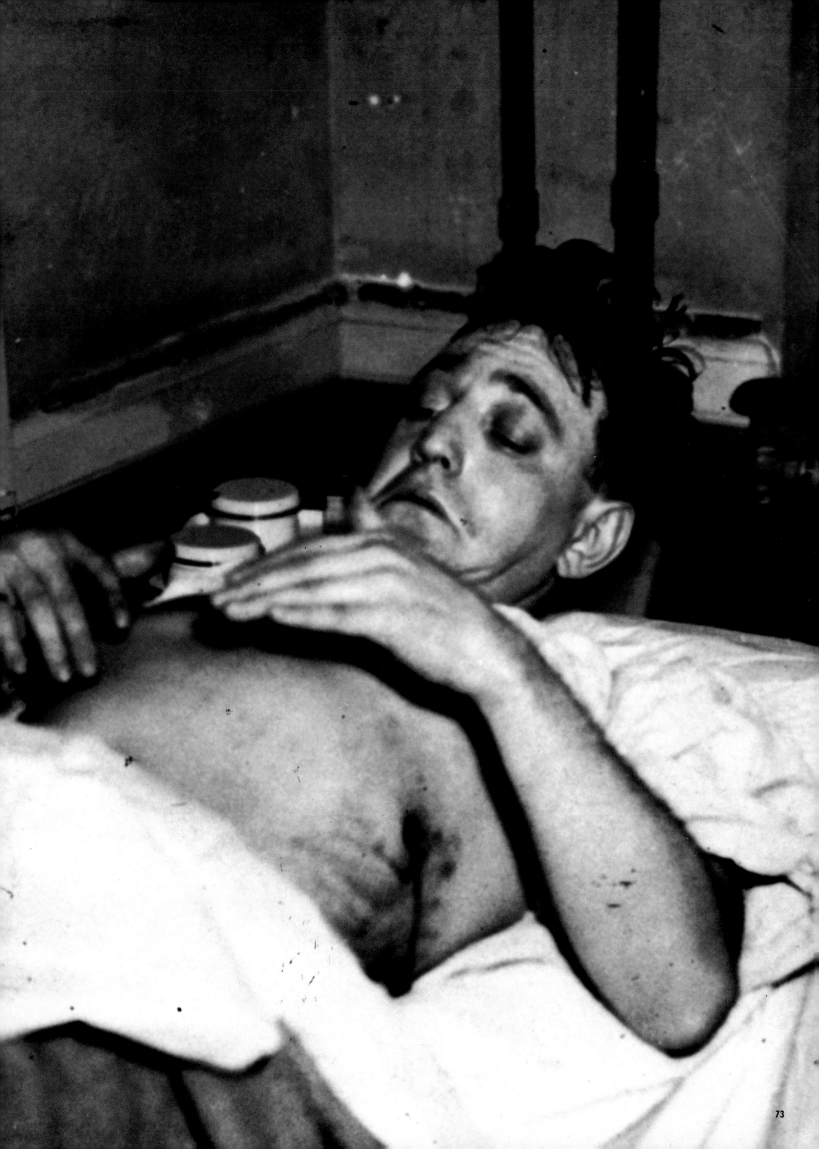

Paul Muni's *Scarface* wasn't much on manners. So irredeemable was his thug that censors blocked the movie's release for a year, until 1932.

...ward G. Robinson became a star in 1930's *Little Caesar* as Rico, a remorseless killer.

Hollywood's Own Crime Wave

When the rat-a-tat of blazing machine guns shot up American movie screens, mobsters got glamour. Defined by such '30s classics as *Scarface* (far left), this new genre, the gangster movie, presented urban hoodlums as heroic misfits. Bad guys looked good, and real-life mobsters began to pattern their dress and speech after the make-believe gangsters they saw on the silver screen.

...red of no fresh grapefruit juice and his moll's nagging, Jimmy Cagney tried to solve both problems in 1931's *Public Enemy.*

Chapter Four
Beyond the Law

So consumed was America by the global war effort—in 1942, these Boston kids got to see a movie by donating scrap metal—that the activities of organized crime went largely unheeded. The Mob took full advantage.

THE SECOND WORLD
War opened up the country.
There was so much room for
black marketeering, so, of course,
the guys were right
in the middle of
everything. They
didn't care what
they did. They had
the trucks, they had
the Teamsters Union,
they had all of these
ways, and they didn't
have any worry either.
A lot of people who
thought they were
respectable saw
ways to make a
lot of money
during the war.
A lot of crimi-
nality developed.
People all over my
hometown in New Jersey
were making black market
money. Not many guys
who stayed home didn't
get rich. How come? Did
they deal directly with
the Mob? No, but mob
stuff doesn't just get
there. Ordinary businessmen
don't know how to do that stuff,
you know. They have to buy it
from somebody else.

—SIDNEY ZION
author

26:—Liberty Bank Building, Buffalo, N. Y.

MONROE
TOWERS

SAXONY

Young Blue Eyes

Without talent, Frank Sinatra couldn't have
crooned his way out of his native Hoboken.
But his meteoric rise to bobby-soxer heart-
throb was not hampered by the fact that he
had well-connected fans like Willie Moretti
(the New Jersey racketeer was said to have
helped the singer break an unfavorable contract with Tommy Dorsey). Sinatra never
denied his friendships with mob heavyweights like Lucky Luciano, Meyer Lansky,
Bugsy Siegel and Frank Costello. His music
reached fans in cities across the country.

Crime on War

THE WHOLE WORLD AT WAR and the Mob at peace. A delicious irony, to be sure, and the Mob made the most of it. With all of America concentrating on Hitler and Tojo, who had time to worry about racketeers?

Of course, if the Combination had been running the country in the '30s instead of just feasting on it, Hitler would have been buried in his brown shirt the first time he showed up in a Berlin beer hall. And the Japanese warlords would have been whacked out by Murder Inc. before the new moon turned on the Rising Sun.

Bad luck for America, good luck for the Mob. But luck, as the great baseball philosopher Branch Rickey said, "is the residue of design." The wise men of the underworld designed its peace with the care, skill and flair of a Frank Lloyd Wright. The price was in blood, but the numbers were in the hundreds. And in the words of Bugsy Siegel, "We only killed our own."

The last of them to die before Pearl Harbor was Abe Reles, the premier hit man of Murder Inc. Known as Kid Twist for his excellence with the knife, Reles decided to rat out none other than Lepke to Brooklyn district attorney William O'Dwyer, the future mayor of New York.

Reles was so hot that O'Dywer took him out of jail and sent him to the Half-Moon Hotel in Coney Island, with six cops guarding him around the clock. On the morning of November 12, 1941, Reles was found dead on a ledge of the hotel. The official word was that he died trying to escape. But the Mob

raised its collective wineglass with this classic: "To a great canary—who could sing, only he couldn't fly."

In any event, Kid Twist's death did not save Lepke from the chair. He became the first—and only—member of the high command of the Combination to be executed by law. In Sing Sing, March 1944. Only three months before D-Day.

In many ways, Louie Lepke was the price of peace for the Combination. They tricked him into giving himself up on the promise that the feds would handle him, which meant a jail sentence, no chair. But Brooklyn got him for a murder. And in the interests of all concerned, including Tom Dewey, now governor, and FDR, the president he helped to elect in 1932, Lepke Buchalter walked through the green door at Sing Sing and, true to his code, he gave up nobody.

Luciano was luckier. Dewey had put him away in Dannemora, the Siberia of penitentiaries, for 50 years on a compulsory prostitution rap that was a frame if ever there was one. But World War II intervened, like Luciano's messiah. The French ship *Normandie* blew up in New York Harbor in 1942. New York Harbor was run by the Mafia. The Navy Department decided that it was sabotage, the work of Italian mobsters sympathetic to Mussolini.

Was luck again the residue of design? Nobody ever caught the people who destroyed the *Normandie,* but the United States government made Luciano an offer he couldn't refuse. If he'd help the war effort on the docks of New York and in Italy, he'd be moved to Sing Sing, and after the war he'd get probation.

He got Sing Sing, but he didn't get probation. Dewey, now mounting his second campaign for the White House, deported Luciano to Italy. Anyway, the Combination had done its work. It prospered while the world warred.

Wars mean black markets. Who makes black markets but mobsters? Everybody who stayed at home prospered: The civilians sold everything from butter to nylons, and where did they get this stuff?

At war's end, Ben Siegel invented Las Vegas, the New Frontier of the Combination. It would destroy Bugsy in the doing, but it would pour money as never before into the coffers of the Mob.

The execution of Bugsy Siegel in 1948 has spawned many conspiracy theories, almost worthy of the assassination of John F. Kennedy: Bugsy was skimming from the Combination and so they hit him; he was crazed over his girlfriend Virginia Hill and so they hit him; he was simply crazy, he was Bugsy, and so they hit him!

Only the Mob knew and only the dead care. For the Combination, the thing that mattered was that it didn't disturb the peace. ★

THERE WAS A BIG
element of the Mob around the
New York nightlife in the '50s
and '60s and particularly around
the entertainers, because a lot
about being a mobster is about
being somebody, you know, having the power, driving the big car,
throwing the $100 bills around.
Part of being somebody is having
access to power. Well, as a gangster you weren't exactly going to
be able to hang out with the governor, or have lunch with the
DA, or get your picture taken
with the president in the White
House. You weren't going to have
that kind of pull. You could be
seen with big-name entertainers.
You could impress your girls with
having the comic and the main
act say, "Hey, Tony, how ya
doin'?" And that was their access
to power, their access to fame. A
Broadway gossip columnist usually found himself sandwiched
between the movie stars and TV
personalities and the gangsters
who followed them like moths to
the flame.

—JOHN MILLER
Deputy Commissioner, Public Relations
New York City Police Department

DESI ARNAZ

JEAN HARLOW

JIMMY DURANTE

WENDY BARRIE

GEORGE RAFT

Let Us Entertain You

In 1959, when the production company
run by Arnaz and Lucille Ball made TV's
The Untouchables, Sam Giancana, the
Chicago gangster, threatened to kill Desi.
Usually, though, mobsters liked to hang
out with the stars, and vice versa. Raft
and Bugsy Siegel were pals. Jimmy
Durante got his start in mob-controlled
clubs. Harlow was kept by racketeer
Longy Zwillman, and Barrie by Bugsy.

A Hidden
LOBBY

The Hollywood studio system was invented not to explore the artistic potential of movies but to crank out product to fill the screens of the theater chains that ran the industry (a relationship that changed only in 1948, when the chains had to divest themselves of studios). This gave the Mob a handy tool for entering the business: unionized movie projectionists, without whom no show could go on. In 1932, Chicago thugs Willie Bioff and George Browne extorted $20,000 from Midwest chain owner Barney Balaban. Emboldened, they went to the Coast and paid a call on Twentieth Century Fox head Joseph Schenck. After consulting his fellow moguls, Schenck saw the wisdom of an industry-wide insurance policy, paying $1.1 million in premiums over four years. When the deal was exposed in 1941, Bioff, Browne and Schenck went to jail.

MOEY TOLD ME WHEN they were young they found Lucky beat up so bad his head was nearly cut off, decapitated. He had a big scar from his lower lip. But I thought he was great looking, 'cause I don't like pretty men in my life. Guys like Lucky have more charac-ter, you know? He's the only one I ever got butterflies in my stomach about. ★

— BEATRICE SEDWAY

Eight years after his deportation from the U.S., Lucky Luciano, then 57, hardly lived a *mondo cane;* the Mob couriered over money monthly to ensure that his *vita* was *dolce.*

Too Much a Ladies' Man

When young Salvatore Lucania began running up a yellow sheet, he tried to spare his family shame by taking the name Charles Luciano. But most folks called him Lucky in tribute to his survival skills while cofounding the modern Mob on the graves of both Mustache Petes and jealous rivals. In 1936, the law finally booked Luciano (hiding face, left) on charges that stuck: pimping and extortion. Testimony from New York City hookers (left) led to his conviction and a stretch of 30-to-50 at Dannemora (below).

Who Put Lucky Back in the Chips? Hitler and Mussolini

Luciano was handed one last chance to live up to his nickname: World War II. Even behind bars, he still ran New York Harbor. In 1942, the Navy sailed the *Normandie* up the Hudson to refit the luxury liner as a troopship. It mysteriously sank on February 11, 1942 (left), allowing Luciano to patriotically "guarantee" that no further sabotage would occur. The shakedown sort of worked: At war's end, he was pardoned and deported to Italy (above, hatless on Rome's Via Veneto in 1949). Luciano died in 1962, at age 65, at the Capodichino airport.

ABRAHAM (KID
*Twist) Reles, who was the
star witness of Murder Inc.
prosecutions in the early
1940s, was under round-the-
clock police guard at the Half
Moon Hotel on Coney Island's
boardwalk. They took over the
whole east wing of the hotel, and
that's where they had their stoolies,
four guys as a matter of fact. Kid
Twist, Mickey Sykoff, Sholem
Bernstein and Allie Tannenbaum. But the lead canary was
Reles, and he was bringin' in very
important people in local and
state politics. Reles's information
exposed the whole murder
machine of the national syndicate. He told who the killers were
and who they killed and what
jobs that he was in on. His testimony sent four guys to the chair.
Pittsburgh Phil Strauss, Martin
(Bugsy) Goldstein, Frank (the
Dasher) Abbandando and Happy
Maione. This guy had to go, no
question. The guy had to go. It
was told to me by someone who
should know, a low-echelon*

NOWHERE TO
HIDE

**For more than a year, Murder Inc. hit-man-
turned-stool pigeon Abe (Kid Twist) Reles's
only view of the world was from the window of a cheap Coney Island hotel (right).
Given immunity from a murder rap for
telling a grand jury of his syndicate's
crimes, he was placed in protective custody
with around-the-clock security. Yet on
November 12, 1941, guards entering his
room found some knotted sheets
(above)—but no Reles.**

A Canary Flunks
His Maiden Flight

The cops didn't have to look far for Kid
Twist; he was lying, very much deceased,
on a landing six stories below (left). His
guards' theory—that Reles, 34, was seek-
ing to escape by lowering himself with the
knotted sheets—was pretty lame, but a
series of inquiries failed to turn up prose-
cutable evidence of police complicity. By the
time the Mob finally silenced Reles, he had
already implicated cohorts as high up the
organization chart as Louis Lepke. Higher-
ups like Albert Anastasia and Bugsy Siegel,
though, were safe for the time being.

The Big Payoff

...id Twist landed over 20 feet away from ...e building. Reles wasn't an Olympic-class ...road jumper, so it sure looked like he had ...een flipped. In the '50s, Lucky Luciano let it slip that Frank Costello had paid cops $50,000 to do the deed. Nonsense, scoffed Meyer Lansky: It cost $100,000.

member of Murder Inc. who passed away recently. He said that they drugged Reles's food with a tranquilizer to put him in a deep sleep. So when he went out the window, he didn't even know what the hell was goin' on. He was in a deep sleep. He went out and landed in a sitting position. And the fall fractured his spine, that's what the cause of death was. But according to Joe Bernstein, he said that the medical examiner was paid off and the captain of the police at the time was paid off, who incidentally after the incident became mayor. They had six guards on every shift, six police officers on every shift. November 12, 1941, he went out the window. It's said they created the illusion like he was trying to escape. It was either murder by one or two men who threw him out the window, because his corpse was found at least twenty-two feet from the building wall. So that shows you that the man went out with force. He didn't fall straight down like a normal body. They threw a sheet out the window. The sheet only went down to the next floor. Number 523, which was empty by the way. Now had Reles really been tryin' to escape, how would he know that room 523 was unoccupied at the time? And also they took his shoes and they scraped his shoes on the sill of room 523 to show that he did make it to the window and that he was tryin' to get in but he slipped and he fell five stories down. They all stuck together in their testimony and it worked. The guards were demoted to regular foot patrol, and that was it. He went out, sailing, if you know what I mean. No, there's no doubt he was murdered. No question about it.

—WILLIAM BALSAMO
crime historian

REVERENTLY WE CALLED him Benny Siegel. He was the killer. He was the punch-out guy. He was everything. When his temper went, he was really insane. ★

— ED BECKER
former Las Vegas talent coordinator

A Lower East Side pimp-turned-killer, Benjamin (Bugsy) Siegel—according to legend—won a Hollywood screen test. Warren Beatty he wasn't.

BENNY [SIEGEL] ALREADY *had his feet in Las Vegas. It was his big dream, because he knew about Havana, about how, in the old days, a lot of money was made there. That was the dream. What made Benny a failure was that he was not a businessman. He knew nothing about construction. He would bring in a ton of concrete today, and when the sun went down they stole it and delivered it back again the next day. He kept paying the bills. He imported palm trees from Hollywood. We understand that those same trees made fourteen trips from Los Angeles to the Flamingo. When the hotel was opened, the kitchen doors were swinging the wrong way. He had no concept of business, and that was his downfall. Everybody says he stole all this money. I don't think he did. I don't think Virginia Hill did either. I think they said, "Benny, get out." But you've got an insane man. Here's this baby he gave birth to. "Oh, I'll fix it up. I'll fix it up," he'd say. Well, they fixed him up before he fixed it up.*

—ED BECKER
former Las Vegas talent coordinator

The Wiseguy Who Got Too Cute for His Own Good

Nobody who met Benjamin Siegel called him Bugsy to his face. The tough from Manhattan's Lower East Side showed his temper early: His first racket, begun as a youth, was torching the pushcart of any Orchard Street peddler who refused to pay protection money. Allying himself with childhood pal Meyer Lansky, Siegel became a key player in the birth of the modern Mob, and his thrill for killing earned him his nickname. In 1935, the syndicate dispatched Bugsy to develop its L.A. rackets. He was a hit in Hollywood, particularly with Virginia Hill (left), an underworld courier who soon became his favorite mistress. Siegel's private name for the long-legged Alabaman—Flamingo—entered the public domain on his next assignment, which was to realize Lansky's dream of opening a legitimate casino in Las Vegas. The Flamingo Hotel (below) was to cost $2 million. Siegel, though, went so overbudget mob checks began to bounce (below)— definitely not a wise career move.

A .30-.30 Pesticide

It had been shortsighted of Bugsy Siegel to squander construction money for the Flamingo in Las Vegas. And though by the summer of 1947 the casino had begun to show a profit, the Mob was not appeased. On June 20, an enforcer crept up to the Beverly Hills home of Virginia Hill, Siegel's brassy moll. She was in Europe. Bugsy, 42, should have gone with her. From outside a living room window, the gunman aimed an Army carbine and squeezed the trigger twice. One round dissolved Siegel's left eye; the other drove his right eye through the back of his skull and onto Hill's dining room floor.

Chapter Five
Out of the Shadows

Mob muscleman Phil Mangano turned up in a Brooklyn marsh in 1951 with five bullets in his head. No help to the cops was Phil's older brother Vince, at 63 the czar of that borough's waterfront; he vanished the same day and has not been seen since.

Mafia Rule

THE '50S ARE DISPARAGED as a square decade reigned over by a dull guy named Ike who permitted General Motors to run the country while a silent generation of young people marched up Madison Avenue in gray-flannel lockstep.

There's more than a little caricature in that capsule, but however boring the '50s may have been, there wasn't a dull moment for the Mob. The decade started in high fashion with the Kefauver Committee hearings, the first televised view the public had had of its fine underworld characters. Before it was done, Frank Costello would be defanged and jailed, Bobby Kennedy would emerge as a one-man army against "the enemy within," Longy Zwillman would kill himself—and the Mafia would take control of the Combination, ultimately making it a memory for the families and friends of the great Jewish lords of crime.

The Kefauver hearings gave America its first TV party, providing the citizenry with alternating currents of shock, comedy and moral indignation. Senator Estes Kefauver, the prairie populist from Tennessee, sold more TV sets than Milton Berle, the wags said, and the wags were probably right.

Virginia Hill, the moll of molls, got yuks when she said she didn't know why so many racketeers pushed money at her. She'd have had a lot more yuks if the country could have heard her explanation in executive session: "Because, Senator, I'm the greatest cocksucker in the world."

The nation also got a lesson in constitutional law as well, when one after another witness "took the Fifth."

Kefauver's klieg lights wrecked some careers in and out of the underworld but did no fundamental damage to organized crime. In fact, the Mafia went on to enjoy its greatest decade.

But Kefauver did great damage to Frank Costello, who worked in the shadows for years as prime minister of the underworld, the handpicked successor to Luciano. In a fit of vanity, Costello demanded rights of privacy—he would appear at the hearings only if his face were not on-camera. So they did his hands, and those hands tapping against the cacophony of his gravelly voice made him a chilling figure to the country—and a marked man to the Mob.

In 1957, Vito Genovese felt strong enough to put out a contract on Costello—an amazing move that should have resulted in his own death, given that Costello survived the shots. But Costello did nothing and, emboldened, Genovese, in a reach for ultimate power, had Albert Anastasia executed in a barbershop in Manhattan.

The Apalachin conference was arranged to deal with Genovese's ambitions, one way or another. But the cops were tipped off,

and this conference became a landmark in crime history. Mafiosi from all over America were found running around in the hills of upstate New York without their shoes, forget about their pride. Indictments were swift in coming, and now for the first time J. Edgar Hoover could no longer deny the existence of organized crime.

The absence of Jews in Apalachin went unnoted by the media, but its significance can hardly be exaggerated. Lansky, Zwillman, Dalitz and a few dozen other Jewish gangsters were still alive and well and wielding plenty of power and holding big points in Vegas and Havana.

But Jewish hegemony over the Combination was finished. The Jews were not interested in dynasty, they wanted their sons to lead legitimate lives. "We lost our farm system," one of Lepke's gunsels put it, more in sadness than in pride.

In 1959, faced with a jury-tampering charge, Longy Zwillman died by his own hand in his Jersey mansion. Soon Meyer Lansky would begin selling off Vegas to the Mafia. Lansky remained a great power until his death, but he did it by presiding over the end of the Jewish empire.

Meanwhile, Robert F. Kennedy was moving into high gear as the man who would scuttle the Mafia itself. This was the irony of ironies for the guys who thought that Joe Kennedy, the patriarch, was one of theirs. The very guys who would help make Jack the President of the United States.

Hey, you can't figure everything, and hey, you can only do what you can do. ★

Democrat Estes Kefauver chaired the special Senate hearings that reviewed more than 600 witnesses from small-time crooks to major racketeers to mayors to governors.

Virginia Hill, Bugsy Siegel's girlfriend, testified before the 1950-51 Senate hearings on crime and corruption but denied she was the Mob's "moll of molls."

Birth of a New Numbers Game

Early Kefauver witness Joe Adonis (above, being sworn in) helped introduce America to the Fifth Amendment by repeatedly refusing to provide answers that might prove self-incriminating. Adonis, who had betrayed a certain vanity in changing his name from Giuseppe Doto, was nevertheless deported. In 1972, the mobster, 70, died of a purported heart attack in the midst of his interrogation by Italian Mafia fighters.

I WAS MADE A MEMBER *of the family with nine fellas being made that day.. People were sitting in a circle. Phil Testa, the boss of the family at the time, called me into the center and asked me, "Do you know why you're here?" I said, "No." We were told to say that. And everybody started laughing, because everybody knows you know why you are there. So he says, "Do you like everybody here?" I said, "Yeah." He pointed to a gun and a knife, and he says, "Would you use this gun or this knife to help anybody if they had a problem?" and I said, "Yes, I would." And Phil told me, "I know you will, Philip. I've known you since you were a baby. I want you to show me your shooting finger. I'm going to take blood from your finger." I said, "Okay." He picks my uncle to prick my finger. My uncle puts the blood on a piece of tissue paper. Now Phil tells me, "I want you to make believe this is the picture of a saint. I'm going to light this piece of tissue paper on fire. As it's burning, I want you to juggle it and keep saying, "May I burn like this saint if I betray my friends." When it burned out Phil rubbed the ashes into my palms. He told me to kiss him on both cheeks and go round the circle kissing everybody. Then he told me to step outside the circle and he told the group to join hands. He said something in Italian, which broke the circle. He called me to join the circle, and he said something else in Italian. After that I was part of the circle. I was a made member.*
—PHILIP LEONETTI
ex-Philadelphia underboss

Cloaked to Avoid Being Daggered

A decade after the last flight of Abe Reles (pages 86-87), the song-bird's fate still weighed heavily on the minds of those disobeying *omerta* (above). By 1952, though, cracks were beginning to appear in the so-called code of silence. While the Kefauver hearings had done the Mob little direct damage—several ranking members were convicted of contempt of Congress—they did spark fresh interest in underworld activities. The state of Washington, for example, launched a probe of narcotics trafficking in the Pacific Northwest. One memorable witness: an ex-addict willing to testify as long as he could wear a hood, thereby decreasing his chances of being asked to do the (Kid) Twist.

FRATERNITY PARK, HAVANA, CUBA   CUBAN TELEPHONE CO. BLDG. IN THE BACKGROUND

o Deal or
Not to Deal

ith the repeal of Prohibition, the Mob
voted all its energies to the three
maining profitable vices: gambling, pros-
ution and drugs. Gambling interests were
panded in New York, Miami and Havana,
here mob boss Meyer Lansky had won
e support of strongman Fulgencio Batista,
ho later became Cuba's president. Most
nerican tourists strolling through
vana's Fraternity Park (right) knew
at fast action could be found nearby at
sinos like the Hotel Nacional de Cuba
bove right). And wherever there was
mbling, there was prostitution. But drugs
ere another matter. Many mob leaders,
nong them Lansky, Lucky Luciano, Carlo
mbino and Frank Costello (above left),
ere opposed to the drug trade. Gambino
en threatened to kill any of his under-
gs caught dealing. In favor of narcotics
afficking were bosses like Vito Genovese
ft). Costello and Genovese typified the

struggle between factions for and against
drugs. Both men grew up in New York
City—Costello in East Harlem, Genovese
on the Lower East Side—and both were
members of Luciano's crime family, but
there the similarities ended. Costello,
known as the Prime Minister, was the con-

summate mob politician who would rather
bribe than shoot. Genovese was a cold-
blooded killer. When Lucky Luciano was
sent to prison in 1936, Costello became
acting Godfather of the Luciano family, a
position coveted by Genovese. The rivalry
continued until 1957, when Genovese sent

Vincent (the Chin) Gigante to kill Costello,
who escaped with a minor head wound.
Costello, in turn, tipped off authorities
about a Genovese drug deal that resulted in
Vito's arrest. Genovese died in prison in
1969; Costello died a free man, of natural
causes, in 1973.

The Mob Bets on Gambling

The gambling parlor busted by Illinois authorities in 1950 (above) was a far cry from the dingy racing-wire dens of yore. As prosperity washed over the country in the years immediately following World War II, the Mob had shrewdly cashed in by enlarging its illegal betting operations. Americans were no strangers to wagering on athletic contests, but sports was just on the verge of becoming a bona fide national obsession and a leading entertainment industry player. (It wasn't until 1961, for instance, that big-league baseball finally sited a franchise west of the Mississippi River.) As the betting handle rose, organized crime couldn't resist the temptation to add to its profits by putting in the fix. That was comparatively simple in sports like boxing and horse racing. Team sports were another matter—until the invention of the point spread, a type of handicapping by which winning the game is less important than the margin of victory. By 1948, college basketball's mushrooming popularity was damaged when players on two national powerhouses, the University of Kentucky and City College of New York, were caught shaving points. But over time, rigging the outcome of games would become unnecessary. As television transformed first pro football and then pro basketball into cultural phenomena, illegal sports betting grew into a multibillion-dollar industry of which the Mob would be the chief beneficiary.

Raging Baloney

Mob-owned pugilist Jake LaMotta (left) tanked fights in which he was favored so that the syndicate could pull off betting coups, but he was hardly unique. After World War II, erstwhile hit man Frankie Carbo muscled his way into the sport and, through fronts, took over fighters, promoters and even one of the sport's governing bodies, the International Boxing Club. His profits soared even higher in the early years of television, when boxing emerged as a big prime-time draw. Network executives anxious to keep their weekly cards filled soon discovered that all roads led to Carbo.

OTHER KIDS ARE BROUGHT up nice and sent to Harvard and Yale. Me? I was brought up like a mushroom. ★

—FRANK COSTELLO

By 1943, dapper Frank Costello (né Castiglia in Lauropoli, Italy) was known as the prime minister of the underworld.

Subpoenaed
Costello to Senate: Drop Dead

Small wonder that 60-year-old Frank Costello was called in 1951 by the Kefauver Committee. Having risen from an apprenticeship of petty theft and bootlegging to become Lucky Luciano's most trusted underboss, he was one of the few hoods of his generation who not only knew Chablis from Shinola but also regularly saw a Park Avenue shrink. Which is not to say that Costello had any qualms about murder; in fact, his personal okay was needed for major rubouts. But Costello's fortes were gambling (following Meyer Lansky into Havana in the mid-'30s) and, above all, politics (he bagged New York City's elected officials, judges and cops as if they were groceries). Had Costello been called to testify even a couple of years earlier, the public might have taken him for just another in the unsavory parade of gravel-voiced mumblers. But the hearings were televised. And though Costello was able to insist that his face be kept off-camera, the strategy backfired: Tight close-ups of his manicured hands betrayed an anxiety missing from his bland, bored recitations of the Fifth Amendment. Most of the mobsters appearing before Kefauver were able to avoid incriminating themselves. Later that year, though, Costello became one of 45 cited for contempt of Congress, and in his case the feds successfully tacked on a tax-evasion rap. For the first time since 1915 and his lone conviction (for carrying a weapon), Frank Costello, first-name chum of New York mayors, was about to do hard time.

Some Aging Crime Lords Just Fade Away

When Costello was sprung from a Michigan penitentiary in 1953 (below), he suddenly ordered his limo driver to pull to the side of the highway. When pursuing reporters caught up, he rolled down the window and said, "Please leave me alone." Fat chance. Under constant surveillance by both the law and the press, the suave mobster had become too radioactive to continue openly associating with the public officials he used to bag over fancy dinners. Four years later, what influence he retained was sharply undercut when Costello had to report to a local Manhattan precinct house to explain away the fresh bullet wound beneath his head bandage (right). A few nights earlier, 300-lb. Genovese enforcer Vincent (the

Chin) Gigante, 31, had sprung an ambush in the lobby of Costello's posh Central Park West apartment building. But though Gigante had practiced his marksmanship, the shot he fired from close range only grazed his target's scalp. Costello refused to identify his assailant at Gigante's trial. Instead, after cunningly avenging Genovese's attack (by, among other things, setting his rival up for a drug bust), he in essence retired from organized crime. Costello spent the years before his death, in 1973 at age 82, living on Long Island (bottom), tending his portfolio of legitimate investments and, from time to time, coming into the city to swap tales about the bad old days.

THIS MOB COULD NOT exist except that it benefits straight society. It benefits all kinds of people. The Mob works. They cause the institutions and businesses to function, in a certain way. Now granted, those institutions and businesses, like the garment center or construction or unions, become contaminated, but on the other hand, everybody is used to how it works, and they can live with the fact that it's contaminated, and that they have to deal with a wiseguy or a gangster to get things done. But they know it works; they know they can get it done. It's just more efficient for people. There's even resistance to running the Mob out of certain businesses. When you have a problem with the union and they say, "Hey, there aren't enough guys on this job and we're going to hold this thing up and it may take thirty days at the pace we intend to go," and you say, "How can we work this out?" they'll say, "We'll meet with the union's executive board, put on another twenty guys." With the Mob in place, you don't have to go through that. You pick up the phone, you call some wiseguy who is in the union, and you say, "Hey. These guys are breaking my chops over issue X." And the guy says, "Leave me $20,000 in a brown paper bag and I'll take care of it tomorrow." That means that your project doesn't loose $250,000 a day for the next thirty days while you haggle with the union. Is it wrong? Well of course it's wrong, because the union is selling out the very men who pay their dues to be in it. But if you're building a big building and losing money, is it easier to pay off a gangster and straighten out a problem? You bet it is. When you're building a building, the Mob is controlling the construction unions, and when you run into a holdup, you call some wiseguy and they take care of it. There's a certain efficiency to mob control that some people have learned to appreciate. It's the way they're used to. In the garment center, for instance, everything runs very smoothly. If you have a problem you call Tommy Gambino or Tommy Lucchesi or one of those guys, and your problem gets straightened out. The flip side of that is that it costs more to buy a yard of concrete in New York than anywhere else in the country. It costs more to put up a building, because of the mob tax. So while there's a certain efficiency, all of those costs are passed on. It costs more to rent buildings because they cost more to build. When the mob trucks haul those clothes in the garment center, it costs more to buy them, because they cost more to deliver. When you go to a hotel and you sit down, you know the tablecloth had to be laundered through a mob laundry, and that the lobster had to come through the fish market and be unloaded by mob-controlled trucks, that very piece of fish is going to cost more. So in the end, it's the guy at the end of the cash register, the last stop, who ends up picking up the tab for all of that, and that's you and me. I mean, that can make a person angry.

—JOHN MILLER
Deputy Commissioner, Public Relations
New York City Police Department

Someone to Watch Over Him

One of New York's finest respectfully watched Anthony Anastasio grab a smoke in 1954 in front of the longshoremen's local from which Tough Tony ruled the city's piers. Anastasio, who kept his family name, had enemies by the legion. Yet what shielded him from harm was not his very considerable political clout but the fact that his older brother was the feral mob executioner Albert Anastasia.

A Butcher in a League of His Own

Less than five years after he surreptitiously lowered himself from an Italian tramp steamer onto a Brooklyn pier, Albert Anastasia, in his early 20s, was sitting on Death Row for killing a longshoreman. But by the time he won a fresh trial, every witness to the crime had literally disappeared—a pattern that would happen time and again during his subsequent reign as the Mob's fiercest pit bull. Anastasia, who co-headed Murder Inc., was an equal opportunity employer (of Allie Tannenbaum, Blue Jaw Magoon and Frank Abbandando, among others) whose only prejudice was against incompetence. When the law used Kid Twist Reles's testimony to dismantle the underworld's killer elite, Anastasia pulled strings to enlist in the Army; he spent World War II serving at a Pennsylvania transportation depot. Demobilized, he returned to New York to rejoin the Luciano organization, which by now was answering to Frank Costello. Anastasia was even given his own branch of the family, a promotion owing less to his management skill (as thin as the mobster was stocky) than to the genuine fear he inspired in Costello archrival Vito Genovese.

Whatta CLIP JOINT!

On the morning of October 25, 1957, Anastasia drove from his home across the river in Fort Lee, New Jersey, into Manhattan. He entered the barber shop of the Park Sheraton Hotel a little after 10 a.m. and settled back in chair 4. Minutes later, two strangers walked through the door, waved away the barber, the manicurist and the shoe-shine boy who were ministering to Anastasia, and began their own work—with .38-caliber pistols. The mobster was shot in the hand, wrist, hip and back, but the coup de grâce was a slug in the back of the head (opposite page). Police found one of the murder weapons (in a nearby subway station, left), but neither of the murderers.

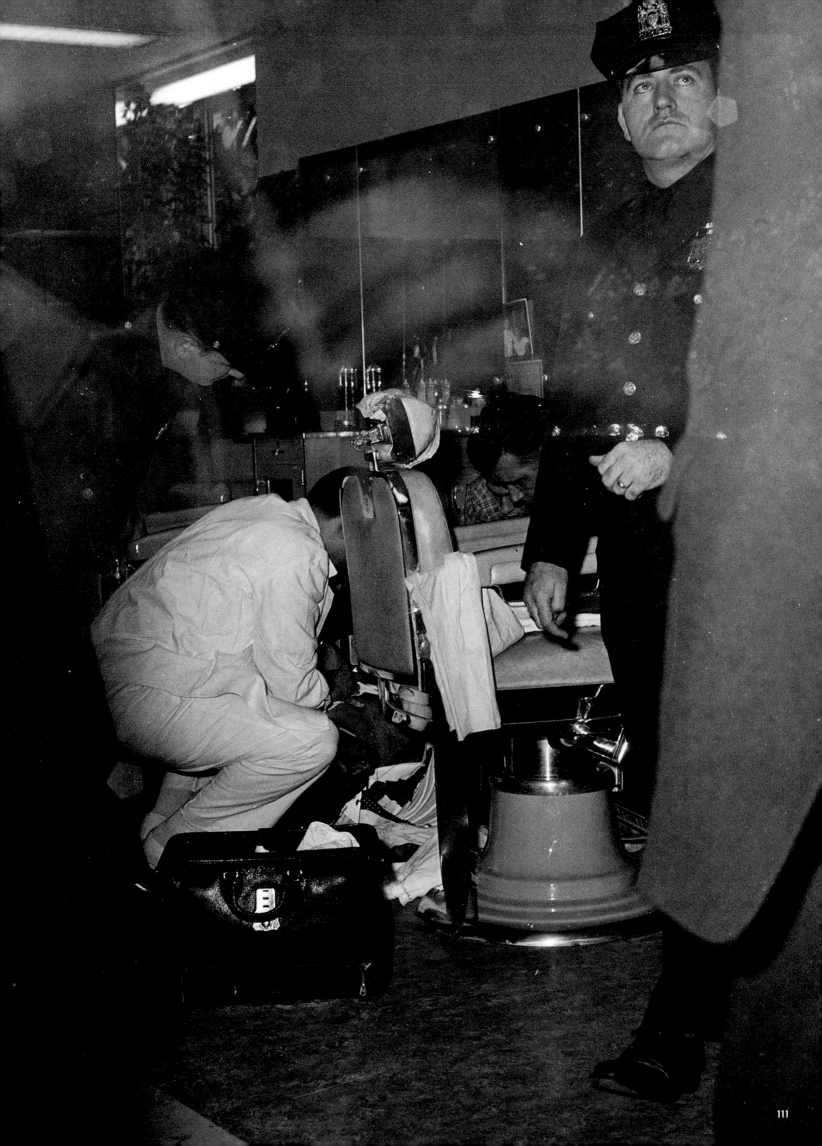

We Gotta Get Out of This Place

In 1956, onetime Buffalo enforcer Joe Barbara Sr. suffered a heart attack. Touchingly, four score or so of his old pals simultaneously dropped by Barbara's 150-acre estate in the sleepy New York hamlet of Apalachin to wish him well— though not until November 1957, three weeks after Albert Anastasia was whacked. The reunion was going swimmingly until two New York state troopers crashed the party, at which time a Who's Who of American wiseguys lit out for the hills. Since most were aging, out of shape and dressed like city slickers, authorities had little trouble rounding up 58. Among them: Vito Genovese, who had come to the meeting to have himself anointed Boss of Bosses; Carlo Gambino; Joe Bonnano; Paul Castellano; and Havana casino czar Santos Trafficante Jr. Conspicuously absent, though, were heavyweights like Frank Costello, Carlos Marcello and Meyer Lansky (sore throat). Smart money had it that they had tipped off the cops to stop Genovese. The bust was so publicized that J. Edgar Hoover had to instruct the FBI to check out this new thing called organized crime.

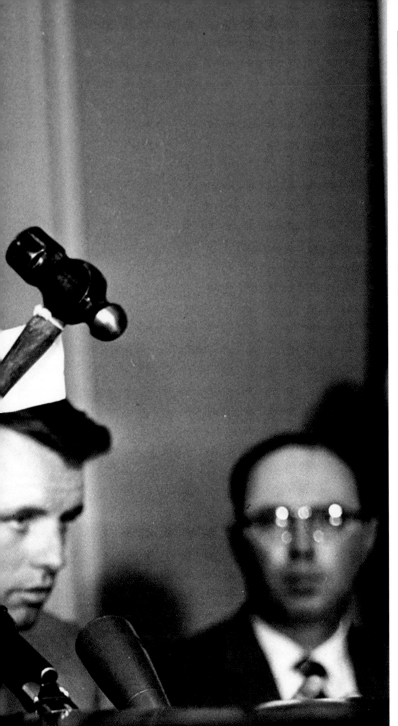

At Last, Names Are Named

The Mob's Apalachin fiasco came in the midst of another Senate probe into the rackets. Chairing this time: Arkansas Democrat John McClellan, 62, whose chief counsel was Robert F. Kennedy (above right), then best known as the brother of a Massachusetts senator with presidential aspirations. The marathon hearings (they stretched over 30 months) were punctuated by enough Fifth Amendment pleas to make Thomas Jefferson weep. But the committee pieced together enough testimony from 1,500 witnesses to confirm the existence of a national crime cartel, and to publicly identify top mobsters.

So's Your Old Man: A Vendetta Is Born

In 1959, McClellan counsel Kennedy, 34, son of a bootleg king, targeted Jimmy Hoffa, 46, de facto boss of around 1 million Teamsters, as a racketeer. Named Attorney General after his brother won the White House, RFK needed four years and two trials to nail Hoffa for bribery and embezzlement; the union leader was in the slam when L.A. bus-boy Sirhan Sirhan assassinated Kennedy during the 1968 Democratic primaries. Four years later, Richard Nixon pardoned Hoffa on condition that he stay out of union affairs. Jimmy couldn't. On July 30, 1975, he met some wiseguys for lunch at a suburban Detroit restaurant. The food must have been awful; Hoffa was never seen again.

McClellan Wants No Truck with the Mob

Senator John McClellan, chair of the Senate Labor Rackets Committee, went after theft of union funds, labor racketeering and the architecture of organized crime.

115

MY GRANDFATHER HAD compassion for the average man. When he came to this country, he knew what it was like not to have anything. One time he had to take a Sabbath dish to get it cooked, and he had one nickel to pay for baking the dish, and he lost it. It was devastating when he told his mother. He said to himself, "I'll never lose again. I'll figure this out to the T before I do this again." ★

—MYRA ALVERMANN

Meyer Lansky's granddaughter

Few mob czars had more power, but Meyer Lansky, the financial genius of the Mob, kept a low profile.

He Fought the Law— And the Law Never Won

Had Meyer Lansky sought a job on Wall Street as a young man, he would have been rejected for being a Jew. The financial community's loss was the Mob's gain. Luciano may have been the underworld's CEO and Costello the prime minister, but the diminutive (5 feet tall) native of Grodno, Poland, was its enduring chief financial officer, ruth-

lessly preserving his power while inventively washing money via investments in business both legitimate and not. In the post-Kefauver crackdowns on organized crime, Lansky's role in developing the casinos of pre-Castro Havana and Las Vegas made him a law enforcement target. But though often booked (in Saratoga for gambling and

My grandfather was *followed much of his adult life and watched and had no privacy. So there were drawbacks. He died a painful death, which was maybe paying back his debt to society. One of the biggest heartbreaks of his life was being refused citizenship to Israel. There is no reason for us to be ashamed of our heritage. We came to America and we prospered to some degree, and we have contributed and Grandpa did contribute. There were plenty of positive things.*
—Myra Alvermann
Meyer Lansky's granddaughter

rgery, upper right, 1952; in Manhattan
r vagrancy, left, 1958; at a New York
rport for tax evasion, right), he remark-
ly survived a 65-year career in crime
ithout a major conviction. Active in the
ob's far-flung gambling enterprises
til his death in 1983, at age 81, Lansky
t his widow a reported $300 million.

Chapter Six

The Enemy Is Us

By the 1970s, most traditional mob enterprises were as rusty as the industrial cities they once dominated. The union movement was in decline, politicos newly accountable, gambling usurped by state lotteries, prostitution passé. What remained? Drugs.

NEW YORK POST

FINAL
LATEST PRICES

TODAY
Partly cloudy, 90-95

TONIGHT
Chance of showers, 70s

TOMORROW
Chance of showers, 80s
Details, Page 2

TV: Page 28

FRIDAY, JULY 13, 1979   25 CENTS

© 1979 News Group Publications, Inc.

Vol. 178, No. 203

DAILY SALES
NOW EXCEED **620,000**

GREED!

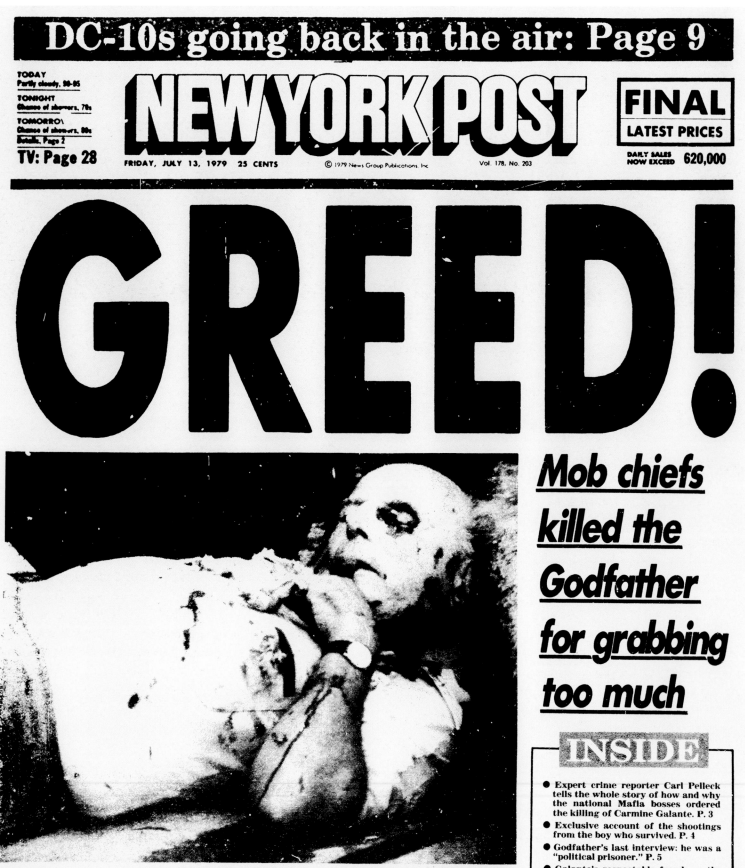

Post photo by Arty Pomerantz

Mob chiefs killed the Godfather for grabbing too much

sly as a detective covers him with a bloodstained tablecloth
of truth — his left eye shot out — was so brutally instant,
long after his life, notable only for cruelty and greed, ended.

INSIDE

● Expert crime reporter Carl Pelleck
tells the whole story of how and why
the national Mafia bosses ordered
the killing of Carmine Galante. P. 3

● Exclusive account of the shootings
from the boy who survived. P. 4

● Godfather's last interview: he was a
"political prisoner." P. 5

● Galante's respectable facade — the
cleaning shop, the ranch house. P. 5

● Dragnet out for his bodyguards, who
saw the triple murder. P. 3

ANOTHER PHOTO: BACK PAGE

Turf wars used to be fought over vice or bootleg; the specialty of New York mob boss Carmine Galante (see page 135) was drugs.

The Evil Empire It Ain't What It Used to Be

ROBERT F. KENNEDY HAS been dead for more than a quarter of a century, but brutal epithets accompany his name wherever mafiosi congregate, from social clubs to prison cells. He would surely take it as a tribute; in any case, it is well-deserved. It's impossible to overestimate the impact Bobby Kennedy had on the Mob in his years as Attorney General of the United States, 1961-1964.

Kennedy came at organized crime with every tool in his arsenal—and since he was the president's brother, that included all the intelligence agencies of the government, from the IRS to the Bureau of Narcotics. J. Edgar Hoover kicked, but he was forced to abandon his preposterous line that there was no organized crime in America, and so the FBI got into the fray.

Bugs and taps were illegal in those days, but Kennedy went at electronic eavesdropping as if the Founding Fathers had given it the okay. He couldn't get a wiretap bill through Congress—that's how different the country was—but his massive publicity campaign paved the way for legalization. Where would John Gotti be now if the government hadn't been able to use those bugs in court?

In his unrelenting efforts to destroy the "evil empire" of the era, RFK treated the Bill of Rights as a bath mat. He thought nothing of calling federal judges to discuss trials; he encouraged the use of highly suspect informer testimony; he used the media to a fare-thee-well to galvanize the country against "the enemy within." His crusade

against James R. Hoffa, head of the Teamsters, remains a textbook in ends-justify-means.

Kennedy's most spectacular publicity coup was his surfacing of Joe Valachi, an old-time Mafia button man, before the McClellan Committee in 1963. Valachi was serving 15 to 20 years on a drug-pushing conviction in Atlanta's federal penitentiary. He killed a prisoner with an iron pipe, got life and decided to turn informer. And what a canary he turned out to be!

Valachi's excuse for breaking *omerta* was a kiss of death administered to him by his boss and cellmate, Vito Genovese, who thought Valachi had turned rat.

Valachi put nobody in jail—this was a Senate hearing, not a trial. But the colorful little fellow with his funny red hair mesmerized the nation with tales of murder, mayhem and general family life in La Cosa Nostra—a term he coined for the Mafia.

His testimony was widely disparaged by experts at the time—for one thing, it left out the Combination and thus such heavyweights as Lansky and Zwillman. But it is now embedded in the country's psyche, helped along considerably by *The Godfather.*

What got lost was that Valachi was doing hard time for drug trafficking—a fact that surely had more to do with his violation of

omerta than any story about a kiss of death. In any event, had the padrones of Cosa Nostra paid attention to the drug connection, they would have seen it as a harbinger of the future.

The Combination vetoed drugs on the grounds that they would lead to long prison sentences with the inevitable informing. The Mafia members of the Combination agreed, and made drug pushing a death sentence. But the money was too big, and they realized they couldn't keep the troops from sneaking. They tried to control it, but after they died, the new bosses said the hell with it, let's play.

The result we see every day: The war on drugs, incapable of stopping the narcotics traffic, has nonetheless turned *omerta,* long considered impenetrable, into a Maginot Line. Joe Valachi died with his shoes off, proving that the government could protect the most notorious canary. Today there's a Witness Protection Program, and now a rat doesn't have to die in jail like Valachi, he can make a brand-new start of it in Omaha or even New York, New York.

On top of this, the Mafia lost much of its control of the drug business to Colombians, Jamaicans, African-Americans, Chinese—all of whom are proving more ruthless than our own Honored Society.

Crime marches on under any banner. All that's needed is a demand for services the government and the people of our republic declare illegal. John Gotti may never get out of jail, but the Mafia has a deep bench. It makes for a ghostly smile on Bobby Kennedy's veil. ★

The Organized Crime Monster Loosens Its Grip

With televised crime hearings over, the Mob was no longer getting attention from the media; drugs, rock music and Vietnam were. On campuses across the country, tradition was being thrown out the window, and the same would soon be true for crime busting. The Justice Department was still in hot pursuit of mobsters, who for decades got hauled in for tax evasion, made brief court appearances, and then walked. But in 1970, the Racketeer-Influenced and Corrupt Organization Act (RICO) was passed, allowing mafiosi to get long prison sentences if their connection to criminal enterprise was proved. It wasn't until 1981, when the Supreme Court resolved disputes over RICO's use, that mobsters were hit with long prison terms.

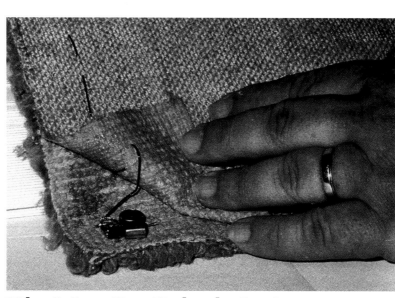

What's Best Kept Under the Rug?

The transistor wasn't invented until 1948, but by the mid-1960s the science of miniaturization had advanced to the point where listening devices could be secreted in heretofore unimaginable places like the corner of a rug (above; the dark "thread" is an antenna that allows the device to transmit). When it came to the underworld, Attorney General Robert Kennedy was not one to anguish over possibly violating the constitutionally guaranteed privacy of those he wished to investigate. Thus, his Justice Department had few qualms about eavesdropping without benefit of court warrants. The Mob eventually caught on and began employing countersurveillance technology. At least the smart ones did.

Putting a Fresh Twist On the Mob

The Mob put a $100,000 bounty on the head of Joe Valachi (right) as the onetime Maranzano goon prepared in 1963 to face the McClellan probe into organized crime. Bobby Kennedy's Justice Department responded by assigning him 200 U.S. marshals as bodyguards. On one level, both sides overreacted. Valachi proved a Runyonesque witness—he alternately chain-smoked and sucked throat-soothing lemons—but since he had never risen much above foot soldier, he knew little that the feds didn't. Plus, some of his testimony was wrongheadedly ethnocentric (he thought that the Jewish Meyer Lansky had never been given real power). The lurid tales did spark further investigations of the syndicate. But the Mob allowed Valachi to die peacefully in prison in 1971, at the age of 68.

A Man of Few Words

Of the major 20th-century American mob kingpins, Carlo Gambino (here in 1966, during one of his 16 career busts) came closest to Mario Puzo's fictional Don Corleone, the reclusive but honor-obsessed Sicilian Godfather. Rival Joe Bonanno once mocked him as "a squirrel of a man, servile and cringing." Yet those may have been the traits that enabled the Palermo native to backstab his way to the top. When Murder Inc. slaughtered the last of his several Mustache Pete patrons, young Gambino ingratiated himself with their killer, Albert Anastasia. When Anastasia was slain, he switched his fealty to Vito Genovese. And when Genovese went up the river because of the frame Gambino helped construct, guess who inherited New York's top family? Much to the chagrin of prosecutors, the powerful don had a weak heart that conveniently fluttered whenever he was indicted. Thanks to a long series of doctors' notes, he remained free to oversee his empire until his death in 1976, at age 74.

Strange Bedfellows

FK had been dead 12 years and Sam Giancana (right) six months when 41-year-old Judith Campbell Exner came forward in 1975 (above) to tell of her affairs with both men—and her role as a courier between the president and the Chicago mobster. Exner, once a Frank Sinatra paramour, met Kennedy just before the 1960 primaries and Giancana just after. On Election Day, she said, Giancana delivered the critical Chicago vote to the Democrats and later, at JFK's request, tried to assassinate Fidel Castro. Exner's story gained plausibility when not even Kennedy loyalists denied her claim of having had a lover in the Oval Office.

A Wacko Gets Whacked

Sam (Momo) Giancana avoided World War II because the draft board found him a "constitutional psychopath"—an apt label for the Capone wheelman who rose to head Chicago's most vicious family while collecting mistresses like Judith Exner and singer Phyllis McGuire (below left in 1965, arriving to tell a federal grand jury about her life with Momo). After Kennedy's assassination, the feds came after Giancana; he fled the country in 1966. Extradited from Mexico eight years later, Giancana was said to be ready to reveal how the Mob washed money in Latin America and also confirm rumors of its 1962 contract on Cuba's Castro. In June 1975, Giancana, 67, was frying up a bedtime snack of sausages and escarole when someone emptied a gun in his head. The CIA immediately denied complicity—even though nobody had asked.

127

THE FAMILY IS A GROUP of people. This was a Gambino family. A bunch of different men that were killers and robbers. It's like you play for the New York Yankees. Your name is Joe DiMaggio and you play for the Yankees. In the earlier days, when all these men were gathered together, one of the big gangsters made five families in the New York area, and they gave them names. Like the Gambino family was Carlo Gambino. The Colombo family was Joe Colombo. But now Colombos are derived from the two gangs of Gallo and Profaci. The Gallos overtook the Profacis, and they combined together and appointed Joe Colombo the boss. The same with Genovese. It was Vito Genovese. Even though these people aren't living anymore, the name remains the same. It's like when they fire a manager or the owner sells the New York Yankees. They don't change the name to Joe Schmo's Yankees. It's still the New York Yankees.

—JOE (DOGS) IANNUZZI
former mobster

WHY IS THE Mafia SO popular? It has something to do with being an urban cowboy. You have this image of men on the loose, men taking chances, men shooting one another, men taking the law in their hands, men revolting against the constraints of society. Not glorious figures. But there's always been respect in this country for the renegade. Will he, will he not, be discovered? All of us in our small way feel we've done something for which we will be punished. So it is a world of risk taking and sometimes punishment happens and sometimes it exposes the

hypocrisy of the society. And America is more representative of hypocrisy than any nation on earth. On the one hand we present ourselves as a moral society, closer to God, closer to virtue. We always want to reform other nations, be it Haiti, Bosnia, Somalia, you name it. Vietnam, a generation ago. All of this bringing our missionary zeal to savages or people who are unwise in the ways we are wise. We're full of it. We're out there for opportunities. There's no society that is out there to do good without wanting something in return. In a way, the Mafia, in microcosm, is the United States government. The Mafia has thrived in this government of ours because it imitates this government of ours. The Mafia is out there to control land, the commodities of the land. It's out there with its warring factions. Soldiers. Captains. Generals. They're structured after the American status system, and what is it about? It's capitalism. What are the Mafia people? They're capitalists. They're mercenaries. They're merchandisers. They're traders. They're into profit. And as the United States will move into Panama City or Vietnam or the Caribbean, Honduras, you name it, you know what we're doing? We're going there to change their goverment. Why? To give them our wonderful world of Disneyland so they can profit and have these wonderful dreams. Well, it's pure bull. But this hypocrisy is as much a part of America as it is a part of the Mafia. So the Mafia really imitates the society in which it thrives. And we are all feeding off it. I'm talking about it. We're selling books. You can't lose with this Mafia trip.

—GAY TALESE
author

The Last Ego Trip

Icarus flew too close to the sun; Joe Colombo Sr. (supine on ground, right) flew too close to the bright lights of celebrity-hood. In 1970, the second-generation New York City hoodlum came up with a novel gimmick to deflect the law's interest in his gang's activities: He began picketing the FBI's Manhattan office. For an encore, Colombo founded a nonprofit group to fight what he called the persecution of Italian-Americans (above). Neither stunt amused Carlo Gambino, who personally told Joe to cease and desist. The boss's warning went unheeded, so just before the start of a 1971 rally by his group, Colombo, 57, caught a bullet (the black hit man was conveniently killed seconds later). Colombo was brain-dead, but his body lived another seven years.

THE OLDER GUYS, *who we refer to as the Mustache Petes, that school is dead now. It used to be very disciplined. They stuck to the rules; they were very cheap. They had a saying, "Keep 'em down, keep 'em hungry, and it'll keep 'em working for you." The drug business has opened up a whole new horizon. Now they were always into the heroin business, but with cocaine and the Sicilian connection and working with the Medellin cartel, the younger guys are not gonna pass up that kind of money. In reality you can't. I mean, money is power, so you really can't let other groups like the Chinese or the Colombians or the Jamaican posse make as much money as you. Or they're gonna be just as powerful, and one or two things are gonna happen. Either you're gonna get faded outta the picture or you're gonna have to go to war. That's disorganized crime. Going out and stealing.*

—DOMINICK MONTIGLIO
former Gambino family associate

Combination Plate

A 1977 massacre in San Francisco's Chinatown (above) spoke to the fact that post-Vietnam, the narcotics trade was in as much flux as America's taste in drugs. Things were simpler in the days when the Mob, with its roots in Europe, processed the poppies grown in Burma's Golden Triangle in laboratories around the Mediterranean, then brought opium and heroin across the Atlantic and sold it in the country's inner cities. But organized crime's market share began to drop in the '60s because the vendors of the first wave of "recreational" drugs—marijuana, hashish and such chemically synthesized goodies as LSD—pioneered their own distribution networks. Now Asian gangs, primarily Chinese triads, were establishing trans-Pacific routes for heroin, a trade lucrative enough to spark internecine turf wars marked by a savagery reminiscent of the great mob wars of the Prohibition era. Even more change was on the way. By the 1980s, America's drug of choice had become cocaine, which had two constituencies: middle and upper-class professionals who treated themselves to a casual snort, and ghetto residents who soon became addicted to its readily affordable crack form. Cultivated not in Southeast Asia but in the valleys of South America's high Andes, cocaine spawned a still newer breed of traffickers to bring the powder north: the currently reigning Colombia-based *coqueros*.

The Rise and Fall of the
Jack of Smack

Leroy (Nicky) Barnes shielded his face after a 1975 drug bust, but the self-professed "first boss of the Black Mafia" was not often shy about publicity; once, he even granted *The New York Times Magazine* a profile-length interview. The gangster boasted of importing his own heroin; routinely flashed $100,000 in walking-around money; prowled his turf in a fleet of top-of-the-line cars; and, to keep the IRS off his back, declared "miscellaneous income" of $250,000 annually. The feds finally nailed the King of Harlem red-handed in 1978. Sentenced to life, Barnes was offered leniency in return for blueprints of his drug pipeline. He demurred not out of honor but because he didn't have one. It seems the junk was delivered uptown by the wiseguys downtown. The Mob was sad to see Nicky go. Not only did they now have to build a new network, but where would they find someone to divert attention as well as Barnes?

Kiss Boardwalk Goodbye

Philadelphia mob boss Angelo Bruno's turf included the Jersey Shore, but the moribund coastal resort towns were of little value—until New Jersey legalized gambling. The racketeer assumed the casinos planned for Atlantic City were his. In March 1980, the Genovese family informed Bruno, 70, that they weren't.

He Was King for a Day

ot-tempered Atlantic City kingpin Nicodemo ...arfo (above right) had reason in 1980 to ...plaud the jury that had just found him not ...ilty of bumping off a New Jersey cement ...ntractor. After the shotgun murder of Angelo Bruno, Scarfo, 51, ranked behind only Philip (Chicken Man) Testa in the Philadelphia organization—and the next year, the Chicken Man was fricasseed by a remote-control bomb. But Scarfo's turn at the top proved brief. In 1986, he was nailed for trying to shake down a local real estate developer; Scarfo's 14-year term was extended to life when he was subsequently convicted for the 1985 rubout of an underworld rival. Life behind bars did little to calm the 5'5" thug's demons. On one occasion, Scarfo insisted on frisking someone who had come to pay a jailhouse visit. The man he patted down: his own son.

WHEN GAMBLING CAME *into Atlantic City, everyone predicted that the Mob wouldn't be far behind. Philadelphia mirrored New York because you had an old-line boss, and Angelo Bruno's basic tenet was, Stay out of drugs, it's long prison terms. It makes people become informants. Also, they had built a huge law enforcement mechanism into Atlantic City to ensure that the first mob infiltration would be caught and dealt with. So Angelo Bruno's second message seemed to be, Stay out of Atlantic City, cause they're laying for us there and they're going to get us, and we're all doing fine. The young guys in the families looked up. "Hey, we've been sitting here with these old Mustache Petes for fifty years now waiting for a chance to make more than two bucks on some crap game on the corner. The biggest gold mine in the world just opened, Atlantic City, and it should be our cash machine, and this old bum is telling us to stay out of there?" Well, in rapid succession deals were made, and Angelo Bruno ends up being shotgunned. And one of the new young turks, little Nicky Scarfo brought the family right into Atlantic City. The takeover of Local 54, the labor things, the loan-sharking, the whole picture. Local 54 was the hotel and restaurant workers' union in Atlantic City, and Nicky Scarfo ran that union by remote control. Every dealer, every croupier, every waiter, every busboy, every chambermaid, everything in that city, the very people who made the wheel go around every day, was in the pocket of the Bruno crime family, under Nicky Scarfo.*

—JOHN MILLER
*Deputy Commissioner, Public Relations
New York City Police Department*

The Sunbelt Gets a Sicilian Connection

Whether overseeing mob business in New York, his home base, or the Southwest, into which his faction branched in the 1950s, Joseph (Joe Banana) Bonanno was subject to the occasional roust by federal agents (as in Tuscson, Arizona, in 1959, below). The Sicilian-born gangster survived the purge of the Mustache Petes to run one of Lucky Luciano's New York families. Bonanno inventively laundered his illegal profits with legitimate investments in the garment and dairy industries. Not content with money alone, he made a grab for all of New York in the early '60s — a move that led to the intergang "Banana War," which raged on for six bloody but inconclusive years. Finally, in 1968, a heart attack accomplished what his rivals could not: It forced Bonanno, then 63, to relinquish command of his family and retire to the Arizona desert.

Stubbed Out

The barrel-chested tyrant they called "the Cigar" came to a fitting end: On a sunny July afternoon in 1979, three men wearing ski masks burst onto the back patio of a Brooklyn trattoria and shot his butt off. Carmine Galante, once a Genovese hit man and later Bonanno's underboss, had followed New York's epic mob wars of the late '60s from a cell in Pennsylvania. Released in 1974, he inherited what was left of the Bonanno family and bided his time. When archrival Carlo Gambino finally died, Galante, 66, said the city was his. Others disagreed.

Green Wave

At the time of his 1979 arrest, Mickey Featherstone co-ruled a gang of predominantly Irish goons headquartered in Hell's Kitchen on Manhattan's West Side. But rather than focus on their home turf, as had their turn-of-the-century forebears, the Westies were so good at killing that the Mob put them on the payroll. One such murder, in 1985, bought Featherstone a life sentence. Mickey agreed to turn snitch and in 1990 took the stand against the mobster who had commissioned a Westies assault of a New York labor boss. Even with his testimony, though, John Gotti walked.

THEY HAD IT DOWN *to a science. You walked in, you got shot in the head with a silencer, somebody wrapped a towel around your head to stop the blood from going all over the place. Chris would jump out in his underwear cause he didn't like to get his clothes dirty, and he'd stab you in the heart to stop the heart from pumping so the blood would stop. Then you were hung upside down in the shower and your neck was cut, and you bled in the shower for about forty minutes. And then they had pool tarpaulins and regular butcher kits with the saws that butchers used. And they would just take you apart, put you in garbage bags, put you in boxes, put you out in the dumpster, call for pick up and you were in the dump. By the next day there was twenty tons of garbage on top of you.*
—DOMINICK MONTIGLIO
former Gambino family associate

WHEN I BECAME A *criminal, it was obvious I wasn't going to live long. Everyone around me was dying. I witnessed a murder and I knew my life had ended. I saw the man murdered in front of me —cut, mutilated, his head and arms taken off. We carried his body parts in bags from a bar. And two hours later the bar opened for business. I saw the look in Jimmy's face, and knew my time had come. Ryan who was there was dead. The bartender was dead. The man that did the cutting was the guy I was worried about. It left me and him. Now, you don't gotta be a science guy to figure out I'm in a lot of trouble here. They were going to kill me. They were going to kill him. They started killing each other. I mean, it got really nuts.*
—BILLIE BEATTIE
former member of the Westies gang

WHEN PAUL CASTELLANO
*is murdered, there's a lot of
fictional and real imagery collid-
ing. I mean, here he is, murdered
on a busy street, a few days before
Christmas. The lights are bright,
his car is gleaming, the Christmas
music is being piped from loud-
speakers, and he is dead on the
street with the bullet-shell casings
around him. His driver is dead
on the street on the other side of
the car, laid out. It's a homicide
scene which, between the lighting
and the sounds, looks like it was a
set for a movie. And when you
arrived and realized that this is
not your average mob hit—this is
the boss of the largest crime family in the United States, the
biggest mob hit in decades—and
somebody, to pull that off, had to
make a major, major move.
Someone took me on the side that
night and said, "Listen, remember this name. John Gotti." And
I said, "Who the hell is John
Gotti?" And he said, "A middle-
level hood from Queens; he's been
getting ready to make the big
move. We think this is it."*
—JOHN MILLER
*Deputy Commissioner, Public Relations
New York City Police Department*

He Never Got to Eat His Last Supper

Many in New York's No. 1 crime family thought Paul Castellano the wrong man to take over when Carlo Gambino died in 1976. Castellano disliked the drug trade; he preferred long-term white-collar shakedowns to fast-buck airport rip-offs; he was even known to gossip about mob business with outsiders. But he inherited the job for two reasons: He had the support of much-feared underboss Aniello Dellacroce—and he was married to Gambino's sister. In 1985, Dellacroce died of cancer at age 71. Fourteen days later, Castellano, 70, was strolling into a trendy midtown eatery called Sparks for a nice, thick sirloin when three gunmen perforated him into steak tartare. Coincidentally just up the street at the time the hit went down: ambitious young Gambino lieutenant John Gotti.

SUDDENLY JOHN GOTT[I] bursts onto the scene. He loo[ks] like Al Capone. He dresses ar[d] talks like a gangster from t[he] movies. The $2,000 suits, t[he] diamond pinkie rings, t[he] cadre of bodyguards. Right o[ut] of central casting. This chara[c] ter was too good to be tru[e.] Gotti was about running t[he] Mob like an old-time fami[ly.] But in a way, he was in ov[er] his head. ★

—JOHN MILL[ER]

Deputy Commissioner, Public Rela[tions]
New York City Police Depart[ment]

He may have once stooped to hijacking truckloads of cigarettes, but by 1985, John Gotti of Queens, New York, had reinvented himself as a raffish mob boss.

Great Tailor—and A Better Mouthpiece

Soon after the assassination of Paul Castellano, John Gotti, who is said to have ordered the hit, was installed as the new boss of New York's Gambino family. Federal prosecutors considered him a tempting target. Gotti was a twice-jailed felon (for hijacking in his younger days and for participating in a 1973 murder to avenge the death of old man Carlo's nephew); a third conviction would result in serious time. But the wiseguy from Howard Beach, Queens, had a long history of making people whom he didn't like disappear. In addition to rival gangsters, these included a neighbor who in 1980 had been unable to brake in time when Gotti's 12-year-old son, Frank, darted out into the street on his bike; according to mob informers, that hapless soul was chainsawed to death. But making even a single charge stick was another matter, thanks to the lawyerly skills of Bruce Cutler (below left). Indeed, by indicting Gotti twice in four years—and losing both times—the government inadvertently turned him into a perverse folk hero. Over time, the man originally known as "the dapper don" was renamed "the Teflon don" for the way even the most airtight case slid off his smirking face and expensive suits.

He Liked the Walk And Talked the Talk

As the legend of Gotti's invincibility grew, each new trial became more of a media circus. When on his home turf—two social clubs in Queens—the gangster was as reclusive as Michael Jackson. But around the halls of justice, he made it a point to be affable to the TV crews and newspaper photographers assigned to record his every arrival, lunch break and departure, and grew to enjoy hamming it up for them (above). His jubilation was usually unfeigned; John Gotti seemed to enjoy more good days in court than Judge Wapner.

From Stomping Foes to Stamping Plates

In 1990, after a two-month trial on charges that he had put out a contract on a union leader, Gotti won a stunning acquittal. Few thought that he would soon be back in the dock. But the prosecutors licked their wounds and began to construct a fresh conspiracy case against the mobster. That trial opened in 1992 with a shocker; the government successfully moved to disqualify Bruce Cutler as the defense attorney on the grounds that he was in essence house counsel to the Gambino family. Then came the knockout punch: Longtime Gotti henchman Sammy (the Bull) Gravano turned state's evidence to avoid a murder rap. Gravano's play-by-play of 19 killings over 16 years shredded his boss's Teflon like steel wool. After only one-and-a-half days of deliberations, the jury voted to convict; threepeater Gotti, 52, drew life.

The Teflon don shows his affable determination.

No-man's-land at the federal prison in Marion, Illinois, a line John Gotti may never cross

THESE GUYS HAVE A MINDSET THAT IS completely foreign to anything that we would consider normal. Our mindset is completely foreign to anything they would consider normal, because we get up every morning and we go to work and we put in our forty hours a week and some overtime and we make our payments and all of that. They look at us as complete victims, trapped in a terrible existence. Their whole thing is, you don't get up early, you drive a big car, you don't have to answer to anybody who's punching a clock or riding you for a performance, but that you're out there hustling all the time. I bet that John Gotti is sitting in the subbasement of Marion Prison right now in solitary confinement. If we went to him and said, "Listen, you went to jail before you were fifty, for the rest of your life. Was it worth it to live as a wiseguy and be the boss for seven years in the largest crime family?" I am dead positive that he would say, "It was worth every minute of it." ★

—JOHN MILLER
Deputy Commissioner, Public Relations
New York City Police Department

Acknowledgments

COLLINS PUBLISHERS SAN FRANCISCO gratefully acknowledges the creative effort and spirit that Carole Kismaric and Marvin Heiferman brought to this project, the expertise and voice of Sidney Zion, who wrote the text, and the herculean efforts of Tony Chiu, who wrote the captions, and Bill Jersey, who conducted the interviews.

Lookout would like to thank all of those who worked with intelligence and speed to complete this book. Specifically we thank Franca Pagliaroli, whose research guided the project at every step, and Jessica Helfand, whose design brought life to our ideas. We are grateful to the staff at Collins Publishers San Francisco, especially Linda Ferrer, whose direction and determination made this project happen, and Jenny Barry, whose confidence and counsel were essential. The efforts of Maura Carey Damacion, Jonathan Mills, Sophie Deprez and Caroline Cory of Collins are also appreciated.

Picture researchers in archives and libraries worked quickly to fulfill our needs. They include Michael Schulman, Archive Photo, New York; Joan M. Carrol, Associated Press, New York; William Balsamo, Brooklyn; Eve Pellegrino, UPI/Bettman, New York; Judith Walsh, Brooklyn Public Library; Ray Collins, Brown Brothers, Sterling, Pennsylvania; Linda Zeimer, Chicago Historical Society; Tim Feleppa, Culver Pictures, New York; Barry Moreno and Susan Potosnak, Ellis Island National Monument, New York; Janice Madhu, David Wooters, George Eastman House, Rochester, New York; William Helmer, Chicago; Dawn Hugh, History Museum of Southern Florida, Miami; Marita Clance, Evelyn Overmiller, Mary Isen, Library of Congress, Washington, D.C.; Life Syndication, New York; Erroll Stevens, Los Angeles County Museum of Natural History; Kenneth Kobb, Municipal Archives of New York City; Tony Pisani, Museum of the City of New York; *The New York Daily News*; Jim Francis, New York Historical Society, New York; Gretchen Viehmann, *The New York Post*, and Walter and Naomi Rosenblum, Long Island City, New York.

A special thanks to Bill Couturié and Nick Pileggi, executive producers, and Bill Jersey and Janet Mercer, producers of the Fox Broadcasting Special LOYALTY AND BETRAYAL: THE STORY OF THE AMERICAN MOB, who were supportive at all stages.

LOYALTY AND BETRAYAL: THE STORY OF THE AMERICAN MOB is based on an original story by Pete Hamill, with additional material by Ken Richards. ★

Photography Credits

The sources for the photographs that appear in this book are:

Archive Photo: 7, 22-23, 26 (bottom), 35 (top), 43 (center), 56 (center), 57 (bottom right), 80 (left center), 85 (top), 94, 101 (center left, top right). AP/Wide World Photos: 96-97, 107 (top right, bottom), 110 (center), 111, 118, 119 (top), 125, 128-129, 134, 139. Balsamo Collection: 42 (bottom left). Brooklyn Public Library Brooklyn Collection: 87 (top), 91 (center). Brown Brothers: 16 (bottom), 34 (top). Capone's Chicago: 26-27 (center). David Corey: 87 (bottom). Culver Pictures: 4-5, 15 (top right), 24 (top, bottom left), 25 (bottom), 26 (top), 27 (bottom left), 30, 54, 56 (bottom), 57, 70-71, 76-77, 79, 80 (top left). George Eastman House: 15 (upper left), 17 (bottom), 56 (top), 80 (bottom left), 81. *Harper's Weekly*: 20 (top). Helmer Collection: 48 (top). Library of Congress, Prints and Photographs Division: 10, 18, 25 (top), 34 (left center), 102. Life Syndication: 102 (left). Municipal Archives, Department of Records and Information Services, City of New York: 60, 61, 62, 66, 67, 84 (center), 86. Museum of the City of New York: 2-3, 8-9, 14, 16-17 (top),

19. National Archives: 17 (top), 89 (bottom), 124 (top). National Park Service: Statue of Liberty, Ellis Island National Monu-ment: 1. *The New York Daily News*: 36, 37, 42, 44-45, 58-59, 65, 102-103, 126, 131, 135 (top), 140 (center). The New York Historical Society: 20-21, 27. *The New York Post*: 23, 32-33, 122. New York Public Library: 48 (bottom), 78 (left), 101 (bottom). Photofest: 74, 75, 123. Walter and Naomi Rosenblum: 15 (bottom), 56 (top right). The Seaver Center for Western History, Los Angeles County Museum of Natural History: 12-13. SIPA Press: 120-121, photograph by Tony Savino, 140 (top), photograph by Nina Berman. Time Inc.: 43 (top left) (Copyright © 1930 Time Inc. Reprinted by permission). UPI/Bettmann: 11, 24-25 (center), 28-29, 31, 34-35, 38, 39, 41, 42-43 (top, bottom right), 46, 47, 49, 50, 51, 52-53, 55, 63 (top left, bottom center), 64, 68, 69, 72-73, 78, 80 (top, bottom right), 83, 84 (top, bottom), 89, 90 (top, bottom), 91, 92-93, 94, 96-97, 98-99, 100, 101 (top left), 105, 106, 107 (top left), 108-109, 110, 112-113, 114-115, 117, 119 (bottom), 124 (bottom), 127, 128, 130, 132, 133, 135 (top), 136-137, 140 (bottom), 141, 142.

First Published 1994
by Collins Publishers San Francisco
1160 Battery Street
San Francisco, California
94111-1213
415 616 4700

Copyright ©1994
COLLINS PUBLISHERS SAN FRANCISCO
Introductory Texts
Copyright ©1994 Sidney Zion

Produced in cooperation with
The Fox Broadcasting Company

Produced by
LOOKOUT BOOKS
1024 Avenue of the Americas
New York, New York 10018

PRODUCERS
Carole Kismaric and Marvin Heiferman

DESIGNER
Jessica Helfand

CAPTION WRITER
Tony Chiu

COPY EDITOR
Patricia R. Kornberg

PICTURE RESEARCHERS
Franca Pagliaroli
Diane Cook
Susan Jonas

EDITORIAL ASSISTANTS
Maria Olmedo, Gerry Smith (Scans)

Library of Congress Cataloging–in–Publication Data
Zion, Sidney.
    Loyalty and betrayal : the story of the American mob / text, Sidney Zion.
      p. cm.
ISBN 0-00-638271-1
1. Organized crime–United States–History–20th century.
2. Gangs–United States–History–20th century.
3. Criminals–United States–History–20th century. 1. Title.
HV6446.Z56 1994
364.1'06'0973–dc20   94-14332
                                 CIP

Printed in the United States of America
10 9 8 7 6 5 4 3 2 1

Page 1: From Ellis Island, immigrant children gaze at the Manhattan skyline; pages 2-3: Newly arrived immigrants make their way to the Great Hall at Ellis Island; pages 4-5: Immigrants carrying their life possessions disembark at Ellis Island.